Please Don't Let Him Hurt Me Anymore

A self-help resource guide for women in abusive relationships

Alexis Asher

Grateful acknowledgment is made to The American Medical Association for permission to adapt and reprint portions of Chapter Five and to Jae Levine Weiss for an example of "Sexual Abuse" and to Cynthia E. Swink Kostyke for "It Happens In Every Marriage", and to Susan Wilbur for her poem "Speechless" and the poem "Go On!" Reprinted by permission from Life and Teaching of the Masters of the Far East, Baird T. Spalding, Devorss and Company, Marina Del Rey, California.

For information address:
Burning Gate Press
18401 Burbank Blvd., Suite 123
Tarzana, CA 91356

FIRST EDITION

Library of Congress Catalog Card Number 94-77911

ISBN 1-878179-14-4

This book is dedicated to the memory of Nicole Brown Simpson who so painfully mirrored the terror of violence so many of us experience in our relationships with the men we love.

Acknowledgments

A book is never created alone. My heartfelt thanks to those around me who sustained and supported me: to Neil McCluskey, my agent at the Westchester Literary agency who knew two years ago that this book was a must; to Maria and Mark at Burning Gate Press for working so hard to get everything done; to Almer Davis for helping me with my last-minute editing necessities; to Ed Moxley who made it all possible for me; to Chastity and Ashley for giving me that extra spark of life; to Damon for pulling through at the last minute for everything from food to an embrace; and special thanks to the many women I met who shared with me so many intimacies.

Above all I thank God for the opportunity, ability and will to write this book. I live in love, joy and gratitude.

Author's Foreword

This book was born late one night as I stood in a telephone booth on a deserted suburban street, clad only in a nightgown, barefoot, clutching my Siamese cat. Madly flipping through the local Yellow Pages, I failed to find someone, something, someplace to call to help me get away from the man who was again threatening to hurt me. I was too embarrassed to reach out to those I knew. How could I let them know the man I loved was abusing me? It was so humiliating. As it was, he found me and carted me home in his car, astonished at my rash behavior. I had no choice but to believe his promises he would never hurt me again.

It took me a year and a half and ten similar flights to extract myself from this relationship. I was with a man who both loved and terrorized me. I knew nothing of abuse. All I knew was that I was unbearably unhappy and intensely frightened. He, on the other hand, denied we had a problem and constantly fought to keep me with him.

I eventually made a connection through a women's center and found the support and information I needed. I went into therapy, attended support groups and read every book on the subject I could get my hands on.

Being exposed to other women in similar situations, many much more severely hurt than I, stirred a deep compassion within me. I saw that what was needed most was an understanding of the dynamics of abuse and having access to resources for survival and healing. No one seemed to know where to go or what to do. Much of my interaction with these women consisted of hours of frustrating discussions about how we could get what was needed to help ourselves in our predicaments.

I never felt as helpless as when abused women came to me for help and I couldn't give it to them. Sometimes, not being able to help meant driving a woman back to her home where I knew she would have her head repeatedly banged on a kitchen table while her two small children screamed as they watched. Or it meant being unable to come up with a home and food for another who, destitute and desperate, sat in my tiny cramped apartment day after day, vainly trying to comfort her one year old son. Other times it meant not being able to answer such vital questions as, "Who do I talk to?" when someone called me to tell me they wanted to commit suicide, or, "He's threatening me. I'm scared. I'm alone in the house. What can I do to protect myself?" Often enough, not being able to help meant acknowledging defeat when women were brutally murdered by their abusive partners while trying to free themselves by filing for divorce or initiating restraining orders.

Women in abusive relationships need help in many ways; emotionally, socially, financially, legally and medically. Because most of them are deeply frightened and ashamed, many of them never ask for that help. Because they don't often ask, we have no way of statistically knowing how many women are suffering in this country, nor to what degree.

They are, however, emerging in ever increasing numbers from the silence of years of abuse in their private lives. What began as a subdued cry for help in the 70's, has fast become an urgent scream in the 90's. The issue of victimization has leaped to the forefront in the media which is now exposing it as a horrifying, bewildering social problem. The staggering statistics, like the ghastly testimonies of so many women, are alarming. Yet they barely touch upon how widespread spousal abuse really is. "It is hard to know the exact figures since an estimated eighty per cent of the cases of domestic violence alone, go unreported because battered women are ashamed, are mistakenly protecting their abusers, or are fearful of reprisals," states Jan Berliner in her important book *The Battered Woman's Survival Guide* (Taylor, 1990) In the same book, Sharon Obregon, Executive Program Director of "The Family Place" goes on to say, "one out of every four women in this country will experience ongoing, systematic episodes of violence within the context of loving relationships and those relationships will not be romantic. Many will end in death or mutilation of the body, spirit or both."

Statistics supplied by Councils on Family Violence, The March of Dimes, The American Medical Association and the National Coalition Against Domestic Violence include such overwhelming facts as these: A woman is beaten in her home every 15 seconds; one woman in every twelve is battered while she is pregnant; seventy percent of emergency room assault cases are women; abusive relationships are the most significant causes of women's injuries, claiming more lives then rapes, muggings or automobile accidents; half of America's women are safer on the streets than they are in their own homes, far more at risk of being murdered, assaulted and injured by family members than from strangers; one third to one half of all male abusers will abuse their children and one out of every two American women will experience physical abuse some time in her life by the man she loves. In spite of these astounding reports, the victimization of women is still considered one of the least understood and reported phenomena in this society. And although an enormous amount of new literature and studies on this topic are being released continually, it is apparent that what we currently know is just the tip of the iceberg.

Please Don't Let Him Hurt Me Anymore

It is not surprising that increasing resources have sprung up nation wide in recent years, though the need for them was already established in the early 70's. "Since 1975, the ongoing struggle of the battered women's movement has been to name the hidden violence in women's lives, declare it public, and provide safe havens and support," wrote Susan Schechter in her book *Women And Male Violence* in 1982. (South End Press) Currently there are over 1,200 shelters for abused women across the country (this, however, is still a far cry from having one in every city, county or town or for every abused woman who needs one) and numerous women's centers, hotlines, crisis centers, statewide referral lines, coalitions, outreach programs, support groups, programs for abusive men and many other significant, related organizations. Along with these, a wealth of community education and support programs, even in rural communities, have become available. National communication in the form of newsletters, manuals and reports, continuous research, reports on changing laws and books revealing ever-changing insights into the anatomy of abusive relationships are flooding our consciousness as well. In short, we are seeing an explosion and the public has never been more aware of an issue that was once swept under the rug, and discreetly condoned.

The result of increased public awareness has created a demand for resources so great that much of what is available is not enough and in all probability, this is something we will be grappling with for some time to come.

One third of the million battered women who seek emergency shelter can find none. Two women and their children are turned away for every one accepted (National Coalition Against Domestic Violence). Blows contributed far more to the rising numbers of "bag ladies" than the (so-called) ill-effects of feminism. In the 80's, almost half of all homeless women (the fastest growing segment of the homeless) were refugees of domestic violence," states Susan Faludi in *Backlash*. (Crown 1991) She also states that, though the homicide rate declined, sex-related murders rose 160 per cent between 1976 and 1984 and that one third of these murders involved men who were husbands or boyfriends of the women killed and happened after the victims filed for divorce and/or left their homes.

The probable cause of this problem is well stated in Lenore Walker's words "...the cause of this situation is not the family as an institution but rather the demise of the extended family and the rise of the nuclear family unit. The stresses and pressures that a man and a woman and their 2.25 children must cope with in American society today are too much for most to handle." (*The Battered Woman*, Harper & Row, 1979) Thirteen years later, the problem has escalated into horrifying proportions with no end in sight and therefore must be addressed by private and public organizations alike. The demand for resources and refuges must be met.

For a time the most well-known resource connection women could turn to was the National Domestic Violence Hotline which has since been disconnected. Though it received approximately 10,000 calls a month nationwide, the 800 telephone number was forced to shut down due to financial problems, leaving women with nowhere to turn for information.

Without informative hotlines, women are forced to start from scratch and work through a maze of leads before they connect to the many services they need. It is an arduous chore that most abused women, worn out and living in daily fear, could hardly hope to tackle. What they desperately need is easy access, comprehensive information tailored to their individual needs and people on the other end of the line who genuinely care. A new national hotline, which would be provided by the Violence Against Women Act, if it is passed, would certainly be a welcome aid for many women searching for resources to help extract themselves from violent relationships.

For a woman dealing with the pain and confusion of a relationship that is destroying her, there is nothing more important than knowledge. Knowing how to identify behavior, knowing who to talk to during a crisis, knowing where to go to get the support she needs should she decide to leave, knowing how to survive and knowing how to love herself, empowers her and can set her free.

The goal of this book is to help fill the information gap and link women locked in violent or otherwise frighteningly abusive relationships with the resources they need to set themselves free.

The sources of help outlined in the Resource Listings at the back of this book are presented state-by-state and include major categories of assistance such as Shelters and Safe Houses, Legal Assistance, Statewide Coalitions, and in some states, Financial Help. Since there are so many listings for each category, not all of them could be included in this book. However, most of these resources should be able to refer you to an appropriate source of assistance if they themselves cannot help you or if your are looking for a more expansive service.

Whatever help you are looking for, this book will get you on your way. And do remember that the voices on the other end of the telephone lines are there because they are concerned and have made it their occupation to help women like yourself. They don't all have the same education or personalities and most of them truly do care and genuinely want to help.

Nothing can stop the flow of knowledge when it is in demand. May this book bring you just that... knowledge.

Table of Contents

Please Don't Let Him Hurt Me Anymore

"My definition of a battered woman is someone who gets beat up all the time. I don't want people to think it was like that. I know Nicole. She was a very strong willed-person. If she was beaten up, she wouldn't have stayed with him. That wasn't her."

Denise Brown, Nicole Brown Simpson's sister
New York Times, June 1994

Chapter 1

Are You Abused?

The word "abuse" is commonly connected in the 1990's with many different prefix classifications such as emotional, verbal, sexual, financial, and psychological.

Yet if you were to ask the average woman today the meaning of spousal abuse, few would be able to answer correctly. In fact, many seriously abused women do not even realize they are abused. There is hardly a book on the market dealing with the victimization of women that does not go into a lengthy description of how to recognize whether or not one is abused. All methods of therapy used to treat those who are victimized by their partners first attempt to define the relationship in terms of, "Is he hurting you?" and, "If he is, how is he hurting you?" Physical violence is obvious mistreatment; verbal and emotional abuse are not as easy to identify. Therapists often go through a checklist like this one, compiled by the National Coalition Against Domestic Violence some time ago:

How many of these things has your partner done to you?

- Ignored your feelings.

- Ridiculed and insulted women as a group.

- Ridiculed your most cherished beliefs, your religion, your ethnic origins.

- Withheld approval, affection, or appreciation as punishment.

- Called you names, criticized you, shouted at you.

- Humiliated you in front of the children or in public.

- Refused to socialize with you.

- Kept you from working or controlled all your money.

- Took car keys or money away from you.

- Regularly threatened to hurt you or your family.

- Repeatedly threatened to leave you or told you to leave.

- Punished or deprived the children when angry with you.

- Threatened to kidnap the children if you left him.

- Without any foundation in fact, harassed you or accused you of having illicit affairs.

- Manipulated and confused you with lies and contradictions.

- Destroyed furniture, punched holes in walls, smashed precious objects.

Why do women need checklists to identify abusive relationships? Why, when mistreated by their partners, do otherwise intelligent and sophisticated women feel confused and doubt their own sanity? The answer lies deeply entrenched in our cultural conditioning. The victimization of women is so common in our society, and has been throughout the ages, most women accept a certain amount of male domination and mistreatment as the norm. It's no wonder. It wasn't until 1895 that the Married Women's Property Act was passed in America, finally providing a woman grounds for divorce if her husband was convicted of assaulting her. "Abuse has its roots in historical attitudes towards women, the institution of marriage, the economy, the intricacies of criminal law, and the delivery of social service agencies. Blame is not easily fixed, nor are the causes of marital violence readily identified," states Del Martin (*Battered Wives,* 1976, Simon & Schuster).

The first book ever written about battered wives was written in 1974 (*Scream Quietly or the Neighbors Will Hear,* Pizzey) and, shocking as it may seem, it was not until 1984, according to Sheila Weller in *Marrying the Hangman,* (Random House, 1992) that a U.S. District Court ruled against the entitlement of a man to physically abuse or endanger a woman's life just because he is her husband. The landmark Connecticut case, *Thurman v. Torrington Police Department,* was responsible for the deletion of an old law that allowed a man to punish his wife and children, implying they were his property. After centuries of men's legal ownership of their wives and children, is it any wonder women have to ask themselves, "Am I abused?" and need checklists to identify the state of their relationships? Even the term "battered woman" did not exist until 1973 when psychologist Lenore Walker introduced it.

Denial is another factor that prevents women from realizing they are abused. It is a frame of mind that blocks off reality in order for a person to survive and cope with a traumatic situation. The atrocities committed against the victim are pushed firmly into the subconscious mind, never sought out, buried deeper and deeper, until she cannot confront the abuse nor resolve the issue because it is not real to her. Denial is so effective that a woman may be shocked when someone tells her she is being abused. "But that's not so!" she will respond, despite her apparent bruises. "Yes, he has a temper, but he's not a monster!" Of course he is, but she is the only one who does not see it.

In spite of social conditioning, there have been very brave women in the past who openly opposed spousal abuse and paid dearly for it, such as Martha McWhirter, who founded the first women's shelter in Belton, Texas, in 1866. Her belief that no woman should be forced to live with an alcoholic or brutal husband caused irate men to shoot at the building. The bullet holes can still be seen in the front door to this day. Though there were not then any identifying labels or psychological analysis of abuse as we have now, the women who fled to Martha's shelter clearly knew something was wrong and that they could no longer tolerate it.

It has taken a long time for women to obtain the support they need to free themselves from abusive relationships. Coalitions, task forces, government spending, national conferences, programs for battered women, outreach clinics, hotlines and new techniques of psychotherapy are just some of the ways in which our society has responded to the cry for help. In the future, women hopefully won't need checklists to answer the question, "Am I abused?" Identifying abuse will be less a matter of contention and more a matter of common sense.

The Dynamics of Abuse

It takes childhood conditioning, the learned values and beliefs of two people, to create a relationship in which one controls and subdues the other through fear and force. Like pieces of an intricate puzzle, they all ultimately fit together.

Woman as victim in these complex relationships is something few dispute. She is pummeled into submission in many cruel, vicious and terrifying ways, some subtle and some blatant. From a sneer, or a cutting word, to the blows she receives from her partner's hands, she is indeed victimized. She never consciously invited, nor intended to invite, this scenario of undeserving mistreatment from the man she allowed herself to love. And yet there she is, wounded and bewildered by a confusing cycle of love and hate. Her enemy, her love.

How does she become a victim? What part does she play in this human drama? The relationship is similar to a dance and it usually begins like this:

Most often it is he who finds her. He may catch sight of her at a party in a room full of people, on the street, in a store or at her place of work. He feels emotion stirring within him. He may or may not be conscious of where this powerful attraction springs from.

He catches her eye, approaches her and makes contact. The pursuit has begun. She, on the other hand, may not recognize him as a significant presence, nor feel particularly attracted. In fact, she might feel uneasy and hesitant, but this is usually dispelled by his bold chase, showering her with flowers, telephone calls and seemingly endless days and nights of romantic interludes. Many times she is in a vulnerable stage in her life. Perhaps she has just lost her job, or has family problems and he makes her feel important and loved, no longer alone in the world. Though she frequently displays low self-esteem, she also often maintains so-called traditional values combined with traits of generosity, warmth, kindness and sensitivity. She instinctively knows his dominant behavior is a cover-up for his own lack of self-esteem and she identifies with it. It makes her feel the two of them have something in common, that they are alike. She feels the way he treats her is love. His possessiveness and jealously are misinterpreted as, "he's crazy about me."

As the relationship intensifies, she turns a blind eye to his ever increasing demands and disrespect. She interprests his constant criticism as, "perhaps he is right. I'm not very good at my work," and his unjust temper outbursts as, "he doesn't mean it. He can't control himself." She begins to believe she cannot live without him and function on her own. Her support system dissolves as he convinces her that her family and friends do not really love her. To stand up for herself, to demand respect and keep her own identity, makes her feel anxious. She fears losing him, fears his anger and potential violence. Her survival, her status, her fear of disapproval from her family and society, and her fear of confronting her inner self, are all factors which contribute to her acceptance of the relationship. She becomes caught in a web she unwittingly helps her mate to spin. There she remains, caught trapped, unable to set herself free because of her learned helplessness. She relinquishes her autonomy somehow coping with his constant attack against her self worth.

The methods he uses to achieve the gradual destruction of her sense of self are varied and many. They include harsh verbal abuse, physical force, manipulation, isolation, financial deprivation, surveillance and sexual abuse. Whatever the methods, his purpose is clear, and that is to control her completely.

This is the dance I have heard many women describe in support groups, personal accounts and in therapy. What is astounding is that their experiences are all so alike. It is almost as if they all married the same man. The pattern and characteristics of these men are almost identical.

Abusive relationships could not exist without the support, encouragement, teachings and laws of our society. Wife beating, for example, was accepted worldwide late into the 1800's. The "rule of thumb," a term often used in our language today to signify an easily understood general principle, derived from the concept established in England that a man could beat his wife with "a whip or rattan no bigger than the width of this thumb." Women were considered their husband's property and a man could force his wife to do what he wanted. Roles are learned first in the home, then at school and later in the work world. Men have been trained from childhood to expect a career, while women are conditioned to support and nurture a man. Myths of romance, fairy tales, the notion that a woman can only survive if she learns to please a man and the idea that she is responsible for keeping the family together, reinforce the belief that women are inferior to men. Through all this reinforcement, women receive the message they should be self-sacrificing and put men's needs first.

Conditioning does not teach a woman that there can be no tyrants without victims. She does not know that her man cannot abuse her without her ultimate and intimate agreement. It is her behavior, her acceptance, her helplessness that enables her partner to continue his abuse. She is, in reality, a participant in the destruction of her precious self. It is not her fault. The fault lies somewhere in social conditioning.

To understand the dance a man and woman create, it is necessary to grasp the complex conditioning to which they both have been exposed. Each one lacks the simplicity of self-love, never taught to them, never instilled. Until they stand separately and undo the conditioning they accepted subconsciously when they were young and replace it with their own beliefs, they cannot unite in the glorious experience of love.

A woman can initiate this change by refusing to participate in the dance of abuse when invited. "Thank you, but no," she can say. When he asks the next one, she too can refuse. Eventually, he will find no partner. Then he will never dance again, for he cannot dance alone—unless he changes his tune.

Recognizing An Abusive Relationship

Women who have spoken out about their experiences emphasize the importance of admitting that abuse exists within the relationship as a serious problem. This may be very hard and painful for a woman because she is almost always isolated and does not have the support of friends or family. There is no one to talk to who could advise her or shed light on the matter.

It would be helpful for her to call a hotline while her partner is gone so she can sort out and identify her situation. In all likelihood, she would be encouraged to stop hoping the problem will disappear and give up on trying to change her partner.

Once she has clarified her predicament, and she knows that his behavior is inappropriate and unacceptable she can decide whether to work with her man at a later date to improve the relationship, if he is willing. Before she can attempt this, however, it cannot be stressed enough that she feel safe and is free from any physical or psychological harm. Whether this takes leaving the home for a period of time or ensuring peace by getting someone (perhaps a relative) to stay with them, no real solution can be arrived at until she recognizes her situation.

The following questions are simple and basic. Answering them honestly will help a woman recognize that she is abused.

Is he hurting me by...

- Withholding affection?

- Constantly criticizing me?

- Repeatedly accusing me of being unfaithful without justification?

- Discouraging me from being successful and independent?

- Getting angry over small things too easily?

- Controlling my finances?

- Causing me physical pain?

- Forcing me to have sex against my will?

- Attempting to destroy my relationships with my friends and family?

- Humiliating me in front of others?

- Breaking my favorite things?

- Shouting and cursing at me?

- Threatening to harm the children and pets?

- Ignoring me for long periods of time?

- Not acknowledging my opinions and needs?

- Not letting me sleep?

- Making me do things I don't agree with?

- Forcing me to be submissive?

- Lying to me?

- Making sure I don't get what I want?

- Telling me I am stupid, incompetent and weak?

- Screaming at me while I eat?

- Trying to confuse me?

- Harming a family member?

It is important to note that partners in most close relationships experience occasional spells of anger and disagreements which later are forgiven and resolved, but a man who frequently inflicts pain on his partner as a means of controlling her is certainly abusive. The most significant questions to ask are: Does he physically hurt me? Do I have broken bones or bites and scratches? Do I feel like I am going crazy? Am I terrified of him? Do I fear I may lose my life? Do I constantly feel helpless, powerless and depressed? Am I suicidal? Does he control me to the point where I am no longer making decisions on my own?

Survivors of abusive relationships have stated that how a woman feels is also an indication of whether or not she is abused. Emotions most often described as responses to abuse are anger, fear, shame, guilt and a feeling of losing one's mind. Physical violence causes most women to feel terror and a whole range of disturbing emotions from rage to despair. Others find themselves impatient and edgy with their children. Physical manifestations such as exhaustion, listlessness, headaches, stomach disorders and insomnia are common.

If a woman answers "yes" to many of the following questions, it would be wise for her to bring them up with a trained professional such as a psychologist or counselor.

Do I feel...
- Responsible for his behavior?

- Frightened?

- Nervous?

- Depressed?

- Anxious?

- Worthless?

- Hopeful he will change?

- Confused?

- Furious?

- Less affection for him?

- Distrustful?

- In shock?

- Numb?

- Worn out?

- Unattractive?

- Afraid to stay, afraid to leave?

- Unable to laugh and be happy?

- Terrified to express opinions?

- Inferior to him?

- Helpless?

- Trapped?

- Powerless?

- Attracted to him and repulsed at the same time?

- Afraid to challenge him?

- Afraid to relax?

Types of Abuse

There are many forms of abuse. Physical violence is just one. As with emotions, most women experience a combination of them. Here are some of the types of abuse a perpetrator may use to dominate and gain control over a spouse/partner and other members in a family.

Physical Violence

This is the most apparent form of abuse and includes choking, hitting, pushing, grabbing, kicking, slapping, breaking bones and using weapons.

Example:

"I came from a very abusive childhood. My father

didn't just push and shove, he mutilated my mother night after night. We had to stand there in fear and watch this. If we opened our mouths, we would have gotten it as well. I remember him taking his cigarettes and burning her arms and face. I remember him taking a hot pan of chicken soup and throwing it in her face until there wasn't any flesh left."

Comment from guest on
"The Jane Whitney Show," 1992

Verbal Abuse

This type of abuse is the most difficult to recognize in some aspects, because it involves confusing the victim to the point where she may feel she is going crazy. The abuser is not straightforward and plays various games to achieve the results he desires. If a woman has a poor sense of self, it may be very difficult for her to distinguish the games, lies and manipulation. Her partner's behavior is often very changeable, keeping her off balance. Some of the characteristics of verbal abuse are irritability, jealousy, intense anger, hostility, coldness, unpredictability, sulleness, blaming and refusing to communicate.

Living with a man who is verbally abusive is exhausting, dangerous and can literally destroy a woman who is exposed to it everyday.

Example:

She: "You are treating me like trash."
He: "That's because you are."
She: "How could you call me trash?"
He: "I didn't call you trash, you did."

Sexual Abuse

Anything a man forces a woman to do against her

will that involves sex is sexual abuse. This can range from demanding intercourse to insisting upon sexual activities such as watching pornographic movies. Sexual abuse is an intimate horror and the pain and humiliation of this type of abuse can leave scars for a lifetime. To be forced to comply with this form of indignation can drive a woman to suicide.

Example:

"I was smothered during sex. I sustained internal injuries. My breasts and genitals were often bruised. I sometimes ended up torn and bleeding. I was forced to model 'sexy' clothes or re-enact scenes from the pornographic movies he rented and was humiliated or injured if I refused or didn't seem enthusiastic enough.

"Once, my husband ruptured a disc in my lower back by pushing me up against a wall and twisting my body into an unnatural position during sex. Despite doctor's orders, he insisted on having sex, while I recovered from this injury. My moans of pain only seemed to give him pleasure. Because of the constant aggravation to my back, it took much longer to heal than it should have.

"I learned to 'go blank' during an assault. I fantasized about dying. After one particularly brutal and degrading experience, I slipped out of bed, went into the bathroom and found myself quietly and desperately searching for a razor blade. I felt backed into a corner. I suffered silently, guarding a secret shame. I was too humiliated to reach out for help."

Financial Abuse

Stinginess, withholding necessities, dictating how to spend the family income, depriving a woman of money needed for health, food, rent, etc. and forcing her to hand over her paycheck, are all abusive. To have no financial decision-making power or to have no income at all and be dependent on a man who is cruelly cheap, is mortifying. Economic deprivation is a way of controlling a woman that can be damaging both physically and psychologically.

Example:

"After a violent episode he would shower me with gifts and take me out to dinner. At the end of the month the credit card bills came in and he demanded I pay them.

"I was eight months pregnant and left my job, unable to continue because of stress. The minute I had no income of my own, my husband became very cruel to me. He deprived me of food, transportation and the things I needed to carry me through to a healthy pregnancy. I got very sick and had to get my sister to get me out of the situation and take care of me or I would have starved and probably miscarried.

"I never knew how much money my husband made. He hid everything. I couldn't tell you today."

Social Abuse

This form of abuse involves isolating a woman from her family, friends, job-related relationships and many other social activities. Her partner may refuse to escort her to important business meetings; he may demand she not work and stay home; he is likely to criticize new friends she may make and, in general, threaten or discourage her from going out on outings without him. If he does accompany her, he may ruin the social event by drinking too much, embarrassing her or making a scene and humiliating her in front of others. He may also use social events as a bargaining tool, i.e., "Do this for me and I will let you go." To avoid harassment, women tend to isolate themselves further, turning down invitations and becoming more and more dependent on their mate.

For those who do manage to hang on to a social life, a high price is paid for it. They may suffer from escalating violence, fits of jealousy, constant criticism and possessiveness.

Example:

"It seemed like he had so many friends. They were calling him all the time. It occurred to me that no one ever called me. Ever. How did I get to the point where I didn't have a single friend or outside contact? Before I met him, I always had friends. I also began to question why he never took me to social gatherings. He always told me I wouldn't fit in, that it was a difference of culture. I believed him at first. Two years later, I finally understood it was his intention all along to keep me isolated so no one would interfere with our relationship, or influence my thinking."

Why You Stay

You probably do not want to leave your spouse or lover.

What you want from him is to stop the abuse and for him to love you. You want him to change.

In all likelihood you will acknowledge these reasons for staying as well:

Economic Dependence

You may not have the finances to leave nor the skill or education to provide you and your children (if you have any) with a comfortable lifestyle. You are probably conscious that men are still the primary wage earners in our society.

Social Stigma

You are committed to your role as the nurturing

member of your partnership and to keeping the family together.

Fear
You may be afraid to leave because he has threatened to hurt you or your loved ones if you do.

Moral Obligation
Your obligation to ensure that your children have a decent life and a father is important to you.

Love
You genuinely love the man you are with. You may also believe he loves you, despite his abuse.

Lack of Social Support for Leaving
You may find the institutions and resources you need to support you in your decision to leave are non-existent, or you do not have knowledge of them. Your friends and family do not support you to the extent you need to successfully rebuild your life.

Hope
You are not able to let go of the hope he will change.

The reasons you stay are best explored with a therapist trained in counseling those in abusive relationships. She will help you understand your own behavior and his. In therapy you will also be able to examine what options are available to you. In your geographic area there are likely to be many therapists and counseling clinics that will suit your particular needs. To find one who can help you, consult the national listing of therapists' organizations published in the Resources section of this book. They will provide a referral on request. Or consult a shelter in your area. They will also provide referrals.

Are You Abused?

It is most important to realize that you, as a woman who has been conditioned by our society, are not to blame for the abuse in your relationship with your partner. You are not responsible for his behavior. Nor should you feel shame because you love him. Those who have no understanding of the complexities of your involvement with your man often condemn women who, like you, are in these situations. Try to do what you feel is best, even if you decide to stay and the abuse continues. You will pull through.

Above all, be kind to yourself. Be merciful to you. And reach out for all the help you can find. Society is finally beginning to accommodate the needs of so many women in abusive relationships... and with compassion.

SPEECHLESS

He struck her once across the left temple

She stumbled backwards and fell and he stood waiting for her to say stop or please or no but she just
sat there slouched against the wall with her head
tilted at a funny angle staring at him.

Come on tell me to stop he said and hit her again and
again and kicked her with the hard toe of an expensive Italian shoe

Stop me he bellowed and began to pummel her, shouting obscenities at her silence her power

Then dropping to his knees he gathers the long dark
hair in his hands though to someone watching it
might have seemed a tenderness, to someone who
didn't happen to see his fingers tearing at it or his
gritted teeth and banged her head into the apricot-
colored carpet screaming say something damn it

He couldn't know of course that the first blow caught
her off guard dazed her for a moment and in the
next split second of clear and searing light as in the
passage of a shooting star left her damaged and
completely speechless

Susann Wilbur

37

Chapter 2

Is There Anyone To Talk To?

People will often tell you, if you are in trouble, to talk to someone. Call a hotline, attend a support group, see a therapist, tell your best friend, talk to your priest, inform your doctor or, if you're really desperate, tell your favorite bartender, but do tell someone.

Why is this so important? After all, it is hard to overcome feelings of shame, guilt, fear and distrust just to reveal your most intimate thoughts and problems. The reason it is vital, and you may not realize this until you experience it, is that it will first of all make you feel better. More importantly, you will begin to understand yourself and be able to make desirable changes in your life. You will receive the support you are unable to give yourself. Talking to someone may also save your life.

Most of us are not able to pull ourselves out of a situation that seems overwhelming and we need an objective mind, a compassionate heart and a firm arm to lean on to give us the wisdom and strength it takes to pull ourselves up. It may be hard to admit that we have been unable to solve our own problems and that, in spite of our best efforts, our situations do not change but become increasingly worse. We often wait too long to reach out and find that we are at a breaking point when we finally do.

The following account illustrates one woman's struggle to emerge from an abusive relationship by finally seeking help:

Please Don't Let Him Hurt Me Anymore

"I was afraid to tell anyone. I was so ashamed. Not being able to define the situation I was in, made it even worse. I was not raised in an abusive home where my father physically abused my mother. I was brought up to have a very low self-esteem, however, and this made me a perfect candidate to attract a man who was abusive. I did not know that until it was too late and the relationship had progressed into a couple of years of attachment. I didn't know what to tell people anyway. He was mad? Had a mental problem? What was wrong with me that I would be with him?

"Things escalated into such frightening violence I was forced to look for someone in a helping profession to talk to. I had gotten to the point where I weighed less than one hundred pounds and was so severely depressed I could not get out of bed during the day when he was at work. I tried to tell my doctor, but I didn't know what to say. I was given antidepressants which I didn't take because I was afraid of them. It wasn't until I talked to a therapist that I began to understand what kind of a situation I faced. I was sure he had a brain disorder. But no, my man was intelligent, successful and very, very sane. He knew what he was doing and could control it. I learned that he was conditioned to behave this way from childhood. He had been brought up in an abusive home himself and simply adopted the same behavior. I learned that all of his anger was taken out on me, that he had low self-esteem just as I did and that he did not love me. He was not capable of it.

"If it wasn't for support groups and meeting and talking to other women, I would have felt so alone. We shared so many of the same problems, it helped me to help myself tremendously.

"Recovering from abuse can be complicated and hard. There's a lot of emotional damage to overcome. It's hard to trust others when you remember that the one you trusted before is the one who hurt you."

Is There Anyone To Talk To?

It happens often that a woman will reach out and talk to people who are biased and give the wrong advice out of personal preference, as in the cases of religious counselors or priests. Depending on which affiliation and according to their beliefs, a woman may be so horrifyingly misled it can drive her to near death. The following is a true account of one woman's experience in the Jehovah's Witness organization:

"When I was single, the elders of my church were supportive and helpful. When I married and became the victim of physical, sexual and emotional abuse from the man I loved, the support disappeared. These same elders advised me to 'forgive and forget' what he had done or my marriage 'would not succeed.' I became submissive and regularly forgave routine abuse.

"I eventually became disabled and was afraid for my life. I felt worthless, confused, inadequate, unloved. My husband's conduct was considered "acceptable" by fifteen other Jehovah's Witness elders who counseled us at different intervals. I began to believe all elders treated their wives this way. I was frightened. I was so sick I often could not get out of bed. My body rejected most foods and was beginning to shut down. On medication for depression and weak from constant severe abuse, I yearned for death to grant me peace.

"After four years, my husband finally left me. My sister sent me to a shelter for battered women where I obtained the help I needed to stay alive. I truly believe that without them I would be dead today. I learned that I was scripturally entitled to leave my husband and that the elders I had reached out to were merely attempting to enforce their personal opinions upon me. It was not God's will that I stay, but theirs.

"I have since been excommunicated from my church and have been in the throes of battling to have this action corrected and that the elders who misled me be rep-

rimanded. I have done this through appeals in the media and the Watchtower Bible and Tract Society of New York.

"My advice? Do not automatically believe those in authority at your church. Investigate and know God never intended marriage to be an intolerable hell."

The message, of course, is talk to someone, but be careful of who it is. You should carefully evaluate even trained professionals before developing a relationship with one of them.

Psychotherapy is a general term that encompasses a variety of psychological interventions used by mental health professionals to help people solve certain emotional problems. Typically, the success of psychotherapy depends upon the relationship between client and therapist and the type of techniques or procedures used.

Immediate relief from anguish and support through a crisis is the intended short term objective of most therapy. Long term effects can be much more important, especially if they help you learn new ways of thinking, feeling and acting so that you are no longer creating what is making you so unhappy. Many of us do not want to accept that we are largely responsible for our own pain and may seek therapy to avoid facing that pain. A therapist cannot take it away. Only we can do that.

For some of us, this is intolerable and therapy is ineffective. When we are not able to face our inner pain, it deepens and continues to plague us. To truly change, we must face it and work through it, not find ways to avoid it. Few of us can describe how agonizing that can be.

There are those who have said healing of this type cannot be done through therapy alone, but that it takes God or a Higher Power to take us there. Personally, I know this to be true. The pain and sorrow I have experienced in my own life was so unbearable that it led me to contemplate suicide. Without knowing God in my own way, I would not have continued to live.

When all is said and done, there is no one who can heal you but yourself. Therapists are human beings, too, and we cannot expect them to fix our lives for us. We can, however, expect them to help us help ourselves, and a good therapist will achieve just that.

It is you who has the final word in all matters pertaining to your life, though your therapist will have a big hand in directing, supporting and encouraging that final word. Remember, too, therapy takes courage, strength, determination, time, money and a whole lot of patience and self-love. It's a commitment, an investment in yourself. It's one of the best you'll ever make.

Kinds of Therapists

It helps to know the categories of therapists and what each one means in terms of training and cost. A word of caution here: as stated in the updated *Our Bodies, Ourselves* (Boston Women's Health Collective, 1993), "Many mental health professionals, especially male psychiatrists and psychologists, have distorted ideas about women based on their training, inadequate information about women's psychological development as it differs from men's and the realities of most women's lives."

These professionals can do much harm to a woman by misleading her in terms of indicating she is too emotional, overly anxious without cause, depressed over nothing, illogical and having mental problems largely because she is female. They may also prescribe drugs that are not necessary and recommend extreme procedures such as electroshock and time in a mental institution.

Sexual abuse is also something to watch out for and, although this is not something most of us experience, it may feel safer to go into therapy with a female professional. A woman understands what it means to be a woman in our society, and this makes it easier for us to relate to and trust a female therapist. This is not to say all female therapists are excellent choices or are to be completely trusted, but you have a better chance of finding someone you are comfortable with to help you improve the quality of your life.

Psychiatrists

Psychiatrists are trained physicians who specialize in treating mental illness. They have the authority to prescribe medications just as any general practitioner does, although they are much more knowledgeable about administering certain drugs such as antidepressants. Because of their specialization, they are generally expensive, and not all treatment is fully covered by health insurance.

Psychologists

Psychologists are licensed professionals controlled by state laws. They are trained academically and usually have a Ph.D. in clinical or counseling psychology as well as training in a mental health facility. Not all are trained in psychotherapy and you should investigate the specialization of any psychologist you see. Their education may not have included clinical work, which means they do not have actual experience with real life cases.

The National Register of Health Service Providers first published in 1975, lists all psychologists licensed or certified in each state and this would give you at least some indication of the experience and professionalism of the therapist you have chosen. Your local librarian should be able to direct you to this resource.

Marriage And Family Therapists

For problems in relationships and families, many people seek the services of one of these professionals, as they are much more direct and involved than an individual therapist. You can expect dramatizations and assigned homework. Family therapists sometimes take the role of a family member and try to get all members to actively participate. Although not licensed in all states, they generally have a two-year master's program to their credit as well as a few years of clinical supervision. They may also have individual therapy training as well.

Social Workers

Social workers provide a wide range of services from welfare to rehabilitation. They normally have a master's degree and are licensed or certified by their state. Though they may practice privately, most work in hospitals and schools. There are different levels of certification and those with the highest level of training are listed with The National Association of Social Workers. Unfortunately, the majority of social workers seem to fall into the category of overworked and underpaid.

Psychoanalysts

These are trained as psychiatrists, then go into further training at an institute for specialized individual therapy. The term psychoanalyst describes a professional who practices the therapeutic approach developed by Sigmund Freud, and this type of therapy often takes years of commitment. All psychoanalysts use a psychodynamic procedure which accepts the premise that emotional problems are caused by conflicts of the unconscious mind.

As with psychiatrists, be prepared for a high cost.

Other Types of Therapists

Since formal training is not required to call oneself a psychotherapist, it is important to know some of the other titles used and what they mean. Here are some of the most common:

Pastoral Counselors

These providers are connected to religious organizations and do not necessarily have any training in psychotherapy at all. At times they may be connected to a school set up by their affiliation and usually counsel according to their beliefs.

Biofeedback Therapists

These are trained technicians who help you learn more about yourself through the use of biofeedback equipment.

Hypnotherapists

Hypnosis is used to treat people for such things as smoking and obesity. A credible hypnotherapist will have a degree in a profession such as psychology, however, anyone can call themselves a hypnotherapist.

Child Therapists

These professionals treat children only, but just because they advertise themselves as such does not mean they have any training specifically for children.

Sex Therapists

Sexual disorders are a delicate matter and credible therapists may be hard to find since this area is unregulated. There are institutions that provide this particular training, however, the therapist ideally should already have a background in psychology or social work.

Paraprofessionals

These are people who receive on-the-job-training at hospitals, health centers, drug and alcohol facilities and other public organizations. They are generally closely supervised and offer counseling, not psychotherapy.

Group Settings

As an alternative or as an aid, group settings can be very beneficial. Many a life has been saved and many a friend made, as the saying goes.

There are all kinds of support groups, of course, and you need one in which your peers understand you and your particular problem. The best places to call for group information are the shelter services listed in the Resource Section of this book. Most have ongoing groups at different times of the week.

Because women who are abused are so often isolated, attending a support group is very beneficial in terms of finding friends, being able to confide in others and obtaining strength. Much support is given to each other in the areas of changes in behavior and practical issues. For some women, a support group is the only social outlet they have.

These groups are also very important for crisis intervention. If a woman is in serious physical danger, for instance, she can get help from the group leader as well as the women in her circle.

It is not uncommon for a woman to be placed in a shelter the same night she attends a group meeting, if her situation warrants it. In other instances, she can get the help she needs to get out of an abusive relationship by planning it with the group. For some, the support they need to recover from abuse is the sole reason they attend.

Normally there are two kinds of groups: one for the woman who is contemplating leaving her abuser and the other for women who have already left.

Most meet for two hours a week, though some meet twice a week and attendance may be for a few months to ten years or more. Members often give each other their telephone numbers and meet outside the group for activities or just to talk. Groups in the stages of recovery tend to concentrate more on healing and psychological issues, while groups in which women have not yet left their partners, or do not want to, place more emphasis on practical concerns such as how to stay safe, what to do in case of an emergency or how to handle family problems.

A good support group is not unstructured. If you find that all you do in your group is talk about the terrible things that you have gone through and find you are not making progress in resolving your abusive situation, you are probably in the wrong group. A support group should be designed to help you heal and share your insights and success with others so they can benefit.

What everyone should be gaining by attending is self-awareness, self-acceptance and a level of trust. Empathy and the sharing of experiences helps healing and you should be experiencing a feeling of belonging, that you are not alone, but there are those who are on your side.

It is important to attend regularly, as it takes time to feel comfortable and to benefit from what the group has to offer. Remember too, that whatever goes on in the group does not leave the group. That means your privacy must be respected. If it is not, find another group.

Programs For Men Who Batter

Therapy and groups for men who abuse their partners have increased greatly in the last ten years. Programs can be voluntary or mandated by the court system. If a man is required to attend a group by the courts, he is usually bound by probationary requirements. Attendance can vary from a two hour session once a week, to two or more 12-step meetings per week as well. Generally a year's involvement is most effective for treatment to have any lasting effects for the positive and many programs ask that men sign a Program Contract and pay a stipulated fee.

Here are some of the key issues on which most programs for abusive men focus:

- Taking responsibility for behavior

- Recognizing denial

- Understanding that abuse is a criminal offense

- Developing communication skills

- Learning coping skills to control anger

- Accepting the fact there are consequences for abusive behavior

- Identifying the cycle of violence i.e. violence escalates, explodes then drops to "honeymoon stage"

- Exploring male and female stereotypes

- Respect for other's boundaries and limits

- Studying material on domestic violence such as films and books.

The intent of this kind of program for men is to stop the physical, mental, sexual and emotional violence men inflict on women and children. Often a woman in an abusive relationship will focus on what kind of help can be obtained for her man rather than concentrating on her own well-being. She will arrange for therapy for him (or together) try to motivate him to go, give him books to read and run herself ragged trying to find out what will change him. So many of us desperately want to hold onto to our men and families that we overlook what needs to be done and what will work. There is no doubt men can change and stop being violent. It is not that they cannot change, it is that they do not want to. The only incentive for some men to change is fear of losing his family or fear of being prosecuted by the justice system. Not all abusive men are the same of course, but most of them have found that controlling behavior and violence simply gets them what they want and it works well for them. They see no need to change. Even for men willing to go into programs designed to modify their destructive behavior, there is one thing that none of these programs can teach, and that is how to love. Learning to love himself and you and your children is not the immediate goal. The programs focus primarily on changing his violent behavior.

Deep in our hearts what we all want is to be loved by our men, not beaten and bruised and discarded without a semblance of concern. Do abusive men understand this? Yes but often they do not have the capacity or the ability to return love. They do not feel love for us. They feel dependency, desire, sexual attraction and romance, but the do not love us.

What is love? Definitions vary, however, it has often been said that love is the capacity to give to another person the joy, tolerance, kindness, empathy, respect, warmth, encouragement, generosity and every good thing in life, as you give it to yourself. To love another, you must first love yourself. Men who batter, abuse, or kill women, do not love themselves. They can only give to you what is in their consciousness. No more.

Although we as women have raised every man on this earth, we still do not seem to understand why so many of the men we love do not love us. Why do we not understand that men who rage against us were conditioned as children to do so?

Very simply:
- they were innocents who were abused;

- we taught them to believe in stereotypes, how to manipulate, to control, to compete, to dominate, to hit, to punish, to withhold, to demand and attack;

- they were not loved as children;

- they learned by example.

And why did we not love our children? Because we did not love ourselves. So many of us never knew love as children either, therefore, we perpetuate the never ending cycle of violence and hate, passed down from generation to generation. And who or what can save us? Those in our society who were loved and whose love was passed down through their generations. They are our teachers, if we want to learn. They know what love is and how to love.

How do you recognize someone who's been loved? It is in their eyes. You will see kindness, compassion and desire to help others. They are the ones who refuse to take up the sword against another. They are the ones who forgive, are strong and wise. They are not beaten, persecuted or wounded. They love themselves too much to ever manifest that in their lives.

The only thing that is ever going to make a man love a woman is his desire to learn to love himself. And you cannot give him that desire. He must do that himself.

Truly understanding this will make you, the abused, walk away from your abusive partner because you love yourself far too much to do such an unloving thing to yourself. To love a man who violates your precious being in such a vile manner is a profound insult against yourself.

Remember he was once a precious, innocent child. Have compassion, then turn around and walk.

For the love of you.

"Relationships are causing incredible pain. Every place I have gone, the most intense pain women were experiencing was about relationships. It is so massive, that anything that came up second, you need a microscope to find. Nothing could compare to this pain."

Sonia Johnson, feminist author of *The Ship That Sailed Into The Living Room: Sex and Intimacy Reconsidered*

Chapter 3

Loving the Man Who is Hurting You

Do you really love the man who is abusing you?

Even if you answer with a resounding, "No, I hate him!" it is a fact most women started out loving their partners and many continue to love them even in extreme cases where they have killed them in self-defense. I have spoken to women who, long after their relationships were over, confessed there still was no other man for them. This revelation often came in spite of the brutal fact that their men had torn their whole families apart by viciously abusing them both physically and mentally.

Loving someone who constantly and deliberately hurts you and feels no remorse is intensely painful. Why do we love these kind of men? We are bitterly demeaned and loved so little by them, if at all. When we are physically assaulted at their hands, we patch ourselves up, conceal our scars and go on to love a little bit more. We forgive, try and hope once more, build, support and nurture, only to be crushed again. At times we risk our very lives or give up our complete selves, bending and compromising our positions only to perpetuate an endless cycle of loving, only to be hurt.

Loving a man who views you as his enemy and whose constant objective is to destroy your self-worth certainly appears to be utter madness. Senseless and self-destructive would be appropriate interpretations. Women involved in abusive relationships are often viewed with horror and contempt by outsiders. "Why?" our friends and family rage at us. "Because I love him," we reply if we dare to state the actual truth.

The most frustrating thing for those who want to help us is that we rarely take their advice and they are unsuccessful in their attempts to get us to leave permanently our partners. We disappoint them time and time again until they finally give up. It is true, we find it extremely difficult to leave the men we love and that the powerful attraction we feel towards them does not diminish in spite of a thousand contemptuous blows. Even when abused women counsel one another, their wordsfrequently have very little effect. Take the case of Ann who had been attending our support group for over ten years. She had managed to leave her man only once in all that time and stayed away for no more three months. Ann's husband had kicked her in the face and knocked out her teeth. She had suffered broken bones and scars all over her body, yet she could not be induced to leave him. Beautiful, educated and sweet, she could have had her pick of hundreds of loving men to marry but she had eyes only for him. As a group we simply accepted her and allowed her to develop at her own pace, never condemning but patiently listening to her week after week. The times she was in the hospital, we would visit her. When she spoke of leaving, we held her up. Did we understand her? Did we even understand ourselves? In spite of therapy, countless books and sessions, the answer was, "Not really."

Some women seemed to have a better sense of themselves and their relationship than others, such as Amanda who explained it to us this way at one our meetings:

"I never loved him at first. In fact, I was only mildly interested in him. What I mean is, it was never love at first sight. I did think he was extremely good looking, though. When he called me to go out and brought me flowers and all that, I took it very casually. It was months before we even kissed each other and months after that

we finally slept together. It grew on me, this feeling for him. I moved in with him shortly after our first sexual encounter and can remember feeling somewhat apprehensive, but I went anyway, partly out of desire and partly out of necessity. My life at that time was not going well and I needed a change for the better. At that point I was already aware he was short-tempered and overly possessive, but I chose to accept that part of him thinking it was not serious. I don't believe women when they say they weren't aware of any potential abuse when they first met their partners. There are always signs but who wants to admit it? And women either think their men will change or it's not that big of a deal.

"It's unthinkable in this day and age for a woman of 37 years never to have been married or have lived with a man, but that was me. I was generally afraid of men, I didn't trust them, so I tended to create very superficial, long-distance relationships. In that way I never got hurt. There were many men who sought me out as I was very attractive and smart, but I always managed to do something to turn them away and that suited me just fine, deep down inside. Until he came along.

"When I began living with David I found I had to confront a lot of my fears about men. It was as I had suspected, men were dominating and controlling. David however, was more so than I had anticipated. The violence, verbal cruelty and attacks on my self-esteem escalated until I was a nervous wreck. I was gaunt, on edge and had an odd look of terror in my eyes that wouldn't go away. I know, because I saw it every time I looked in the mirror. Bruises and scratches more often than not, were apparent on my back, legs and arms. I was appalled at the sight of myself.

"I stayed with this man for over three years. I grew to love him very much although I hated what he did to me when he was abusive. We were very much alike in many ways, passionate, emotional, intelligent, sociable,

*ambitious, strong-willed and affectionate. We had simi-
lar interests and attitudes. We learned from each other
in the areas we differed. We also shared similar family
backgrounds. Neither one of us had been loved by our
parents and were basically criticized and neglected as
children. But we differed a great deal in such things as
tolerance, generosity, trust and communication skills.*

*"Loving him had very little to do with whether he
loved me or not. I loved him because I understood him.
His anger, criticism and violent rages towards me were
not acceptable, but I understood. The way he treated me
was the way he treated himself on the inside. The way
he talked to me was the way he talked to himself. He
didn't trust himself, so he didn't trust me. He couldn't
communicate with himself about his deepest feelings,
therefore he couldn't talk to me. If there was something
about me he didn't like or approve of, it was the same
thing he was afraid he had. When he hurt me, he hurt
himself just as much. The only way he could live with it
was to block it from his mind and not acknowledge it. As
a result, therapy was out of the question for him because
as far as he was concerned, he didn't have a problem.*

*"In the end, I accepted him for what he was. I just
let him be what he was without trying to change him. I
didn't hate him or condemn him. Not trying to change
him was an enlightening thing. I began to focus on me
and let myself love me. Instead of trying to help him, I
began to help myself. Out of love for myself, I left him. I
didn't leave him because I hated him or wanted to hurt
him. I never stopped loving him, I started loving myself.*

*"Have you ever heard the saying, 'Every woman
loves a bastard sometime in her life?' Well, what does it
mean? How can you love a bastard? I think the answer
is, the man is not entirely a bastard. And when you have
an understanding of why he became one, I think you
could weep. Everything the man I loved did to me, (and
more) was first done to him by his parents and his envi-*

ronment when he was a child. *Understanding this does not make it right, nor excuse him for his abuse, but understanding allows you to forgive and feel compassion. When you understand, you can walk away and not feel the desire to return.*

"If you love yourself, living with a man who abuses you is out of the question. Loving him is not. Unless he learns to love himself and resolve his anger and pain, you can only love him from afar. In my case, I chose to leave so I could love another man who already had the ability to love."

Other women in the same group had other answers. Elizabeth for instance, simply stated, *"He's a good man. He loves me."* Carol on the other hand said, *"He sent me flowers, gave me wonderful presents and wrote romantic notes to me. He promised me the world, no kidding. He wanted me so much. I felt as if I had found the love of my life. He was so much fun and it was all so romantic. I had so much hope then. This was at the beginning of our relationship. He made me feel loved like no one else ever did. I can't forget that part of him and that is why I can't let go."*

Joni, a woman of 29 who had been with her man for almost eight years was so anxious and underweight (a scant ninety pounds) people around her feared for her health. Her husband's infidelity caused her such pain she could not eat. Yet she had this to say about him. *"How do you put a feeling into words? I feel warm and safe when I am in his arms. His body is soft and his touch is gentle. Who can tell me in that moment I am not loved? Who can not see why I love him? This man who has warred with me, does he bring me joy? Indeed he does. Does he love me? In those moments, I feel spectacularly loved."*

Thea Dubow, who was convicted of killing her husband with a gun, once said, *"If the terror, fear, humiliation and degradation had been constant, I would like to*

Please Don't Let Him Hurt Me Anymore

think I would have left him immediately. But there were also long periods when Abbie was loving, when he would lavish me with flowers, trips, clothes and jewelry. I kept trying to be a different, loving wife so that he would continue to be that charming, marvelous guy. But, no matter how hard I tried something eventually sparked his abuse. And just as predictably, after he beat me he would change again from dreadful to wonderful, and I would deny the reality of his cruel behavior." (New Woman, 1992)

I never met an abused woman who could not identify with Thea Dubow's words.

If you say you love your man, then certainly no one can dispute that you do. After all, you know what love is for yourself, what you feel. No one else can feel what you do. But have you ever asked yourself why you feel this way? Or why you feel this way about him but not another man? Have you ever wondered what it would be like to be loved all the time, not just in moments or bits and pieces? Imagine feeling anticipation instead of anxiety every time you hear his car in the driveway. "Dad's home!" you call to the kids and they run out to meet him with glee. Imagine not ever being sworn at, or having a good old fashioned argument without fear of being terrorized. Imagine getting flowers for no other reason than just because you are you, not because he wants you to forgive him for pushing you around the night before. And wouldn't it feel exhilarating to be respected for your opinions instead of condemned? Imagine the man you love being proud of you at social outings instead of demeaning you in public. Imagine feeling able to draw close to him at night, knowing he is your best friend instead of a potential, explosive enemy. Imagine him treating you like you treat him, with kindness, understanding, concern and affection. And think what it would be like to never have to conceal him or his behavior from your friends and family. How wonderful it would be to relax in your own home, to never have to worry that he is not being honest with you, to know he is beside you to face the world no matter what happens. Imagine not feeling abandond, not yearning for those special moments of love, no more struggling to try and make it right, no more sneaking to hide things he doesn't like, no more walking on eggshells, no more bending backwards to please, no more compromising your deepest essence. Imagine looking into his eyes and seeing a sparkle of humor and affection there. Eyes that speak to you with approval, happiness and desire? Eyes that would never hurt you.

Some women might read this and be amused for they live life no other way and could not imagine what it would be like to live a life like yours. They could not relate to being abused in any way. It is not to say their lives are perfect or that there are never any conflicts in their relationships, but fundamentally they are loved and respected by the men they are with. Just as you may think such a life is a dream, surely your relationship is an unreal nightmare to them. You've never been loved. They've never been abused. And if you don't believe women live these lives, look at the statistics. If one woman in two will be abused at some time in her life by the man with whom she is intimate, that means at least half of us are treated well by the men we love, if the statistics are correct. Which woman would you like to be? It's not a dream. It's real. To be loved in a healthy, relaxed way by the man of your choice is a reality.

So why are you loving a man who mistreats you?

Are you stupid? Are you blind? Not likely. I am sure that you see perfectly well what is happening and what he is doing to you. Your logical mind is working. You think along these lines..."My God, this is humiliating. I've got a black eye. What will my friends at the office say? What if my parents find out? They're all going to say he doesn't love me and ask me what kind of an idiot I am to have married him. I don't want to leave him. I've got to make this right. As soon as I get over the shock of it, I'll figure out what to do. In the meantime, I won't let anyone know." This is fairly typical of a woman's response when she is first hurt by the man she loves. Most women I spoke to really understood why they felt such an overwhelming desire for the man who abused them.

Feelings

The reasons why we are with a particular person remain vague for most of us. It's usually a physical attraction combined with very strong feelings. We feel excited to be with our partners, sad without them, romantic, happy, nervous—a whole spectrum of feelings. Some of these feelings can appear to have very little do with logic or the reasoning part of our brains. It is of little use to tell us that "you don't love yourself and that is why you are involved in an abusive relationship." What does that really mean? Our reasoning tells us that we should not be mistreated, it is not good for us and it makes us unhappy and, at times, frightened. That is clear. Though many of us go into denial, somewhere along the line, we acknowledge that this abuse is a negative attack against ourselves. So why are we reluctant to get out of the relationship? We don't want to leave even though it makes no sense. We love him, we say. It's our feelings that keep us there.

Most of the women I met told me it took them years to leave, if they left at all. Once in a while I would meet someone who actually got out very quickly, but most women don't. Without exception, when asked why they loved their partner or stayed with them, the answer always referred to how they felt. "I feel so lonely without him," or "I'm afraid to leave," or I have these feelings of longing for him."

What I found so remarkable was that so often these feelings did not correspond to reality. They were not logical. It was as if the two were at odds with each other. The more aware I became of my own feelings and those of women involved with men who were mistreating them, the more clearly I saw these emotions could not be controlled by reasoning them out. For example, some of us had feelings of guilt after we experienced an abusive episode. Why would we feel guilt for another's obvious wrongdoing? It was all backwards. Some of us were prone to feeling exceptionally sad and had tremendous emotions of loss after a demeaning, vicious attack by our partners. Wasn't it reasonable to feel indignant and angry? Why miss someone who slams you into a wall? It didn't seem to make any difference how violent the abuse was. Broken bones, dead pets, missing hair, shattered spirits-nothing stopped the feelings of attraction, affection and bonding. In spite of the tremendous amount of pain and suffering women went through, they were reluctant to leave. Wouldn't a rational mind feel relief at the thought of leaving? What kind of human being wouldn't want to escape from a brutal persecutor? The truth is, some women, even after managing to break free from the abusive men they loved, felt disappointment and regret and yearned to be with them again.

Helpless to explain to ourselves and to others the "why" of loving men who abuse us, we shun society, lose our friends and become estranged from our families. We isolate ourselves (with our partner's help) and feel hopeless. We have difficulty accepting our own behavior and suffer from low self-esteem. Certainly, no one admires us. Our mothers wail about the situation and we recall the words of our best friend, "Leave the jerk. You're too good for him. You can do better than that." Silently we agree but find ourselves unable to change how we feel, no matter how often we try.

Watching a woman go through the throes of such a tragic situation is pure agony, especially if you love her as your friend or relative. In spite of the fact that I was involved in my own negative creation with a man, I could not bear to watch my best friend in hers. I loathed the way her husband treated her. He was so smug, so condescending, so cruel and demeaning. He controlled her to the point she was a walking zombie, thin and pale and completely unwilling to make a decision about anything without considering him. She was a beautiful woman of 26 when she met him. With a college education, a sharp wit, a brave and daring personality, she could excel in anything she chose. She loved advertising sales but after a few years with her abuser, she dwindled down to a filing clerk in an office. He was only four years older than she, born in Central America, uneducated, a brazen macho brute. With him she lived in the ghetto, allowed him to isolate her from her family and race, absorbed her being in filth and values that were completely alien to her. Her husband, for example, knew that his brother, with whom they lived, was infected with the AIDS virus, but never told her until the man was admitted to the hospital and died. She gave him her money, her heart and soul, her very self. He struck her, swore at her, tried to convince her she was white trash and threatened her physically if she dared to do something he did not like. I begged her to leave. She would not. No amount of reasoning could get her to leave him. It tore me apart because she was so special to me and I did not want to see her suffer. It was only when she was seven months pregnant and could hardly stand on her feet, she came to me. Between the two of us we nursed her back to optimum health in the nick of time enabling her to give birth to an astounding, alert and gorgeous baby girl. She revealed to me that her husband had been deliberately trying to starve her to hurt her and the baby. She wasn't working at the time and did not have access to her own money. Still, after all we went through, she went back to him. A year later she left permanently and I was happy to help her do so. It was her child that prompted this action. Watching her and others taught me much about myself and I began to understand a very basic characteristic of women who in relationships with abusive men:

Their feelings do not match their reality.

A woman who was beaten in the face with a sledge-hammer stated, "I thought he loved me. That's why I stayed." Another severely beaten woman said, "I was afraid to leave." The answers women gave to the question, "Why do you stay?" were so illogical it was bewildering. How can a woman be afraid to leave? A rational mind would be too afraid to stay. How can a woman say that "He loves me," after she is marred by her partner with a sledgehammer? Where did these strange interpretations come from, I wondered. It was then I began to explore "programming."

Programming

I had often heard the term "programming" in therapy and read about in books. But, I never really understood it until I began probing into my own behavior and the feelings that lay behind that behavior. From what I could tell, most women in abusive relationships did not grasp the meaning of it either, or did not even know of the term.

Programming is a process of conditioning that results in an automatic, and usually subconscious emotional response to a given object, entity, situation or statement.

When you were a child you accepted attitudes, opinions and beliefs about yourself from adults around you. These were repeated over and over, causing you to respond with certain feelings. You did this because as a child you were vulnerable. You saw your parents and other adults as powerful and all knowing. You were afraid of them and needed them. You also wanted to be loved by them. For example, if you had a parent who constantly told you that you were ugly and worthless, you acquired the feeling of self-hate. It did not matter that you were beautiful. As you grew up, the feeling became so familiar and ingrained, you were not really aware of it anymore. As an adult, all you know is that you feel "ugly." You may look in the mirror and see a very pretty face but the moment you walk away from it, you feel ugly. You will attract people who have a need to belittle you by telling you that you are unattractive so they can feel better about themselves. You will attract those who are not attractive at all, even though you, in fact, are attractive. You will feel insecure and go through great effort to make yourself beautiful. Nothing works. You know you are good looking because you have eyes and furthermore, some people have told you so. But you continue to feel ugly. Your emotions are not in sync with your reasoning. Your emotions do not listen to logic.

Programming is a very, very subtle thing. If you want to discover what your programming is, you must learn to watch and listen to yourself very carefully. You must become conscious of your feelings. Emotions that come from negative programming usually feel uncomfortable and unnatural, though familiar. They rarely make sense. If you have just bought a new dress for instance, and you love it and you go out in it and someone comes up to you and tells you they adore it and you find yourself saying, "Oh, this thing? It's all right," you know you are in your programming. You come out of your trance the moment the person leaves and you feel awful. Why did you say that? You loved your dress. You weren't responding to reality, you were responding to your emotions. These emotions cause you to behave in ways that are not appropriate to the situation.

The reason you love a man who abuses you is because you were programmed as a child to do so.

Loving the Man Who is Hurting You

When I first allowed this statement to enter my head I immediately scoffed at it. No one had ever hit me in my life. I was never sworn at. My father never hit my mother. I never knew a single battered woman nor did I even know the term. Eventually, however, I had to explore the concept of programming because I could not figure out why I was behaving the way I was. I kept wanting to go back to the man who abused me. I loved him, in fact.

As I became sensitive to myself I began to notice things. Face to face with my partner, I had absolutely no recollection of the previous abusive incident he put me through. When he was away from me, I would start thinking about it and become justifiably angry and frightened telling myself to get away from him. The moment I heard his voice I "forgot" all about it. I felt so loving towards him. Later on I would say to myself, "But don't you remember what he did to you last week? How can you be so attracted to him? You're leg is still bruised!" I allowed him to mistreat me and get away with it all because I had this loving feeling. It took enormous effort and time for me to figure out that my partner in essence, was a combination of my mother and father. He treated me like my parents did. He talked to me the same way they did. He glared at me in the identical way my parents had. After verbally ripping me apart until I was in tears, he told me he loved me, just like my parents did when I was a child. He was aloof and wouldn't acknowledge my talents, just as my father never had. It wasn't that he said everything they did word for word, but his predominant attitude towards me was the same. It was an incredible revelation when I finally became conscious of my feelings and behavior. In many ways I was the same person with him that I had been as a child with my family. Through the years, I really hadn't changed very much at all.

It took absolute will power to admit that my parents not only never loved me, but they never really liked me. It hurt me deeply. Incidents of violence and threats

67

came back into my memory, things I had so adeptly forgotten. It was my mother who beat us with a wooden spoon, threw glasses and scissors at us and who hated me without reason. My father didn't really stand up for me or my siblings, he let her do her damage. I felt like a failure, a nobody all my life because of the messages I absorbed from my parents. And the man I was with was simply a willing extension of them.

"Psychotherapists know how badly our field needs specific procedures for transforming a poor self-concept, "wrote Nathaniel Branden in his book, *How To Raise Your Self-Esteem*. (Bantam, 1987) Practical, workable methods to change the way you *feel* are still being researched today and new approaches continually make an impact on many troubled lives, however it takes time, money and great effort to apply them to your daily life. What worked for me is the following simple action:

To change how you feel in a given situation, do not act on the feeling that is causing the behavior that is harming you. Stop reinforcing it. Don't push the buttons that cause it. Separate the feeling from the behavior. Divide and conquer.

This does not mean repressing your feelings or going into denial. It means becoming conscious and deliberately not acting on your emotions. Do you want to stop being attracted to men who are abusive? Do you want to stop desiring your present abusive partner? If so, when you feel the feelings of desire for the person, do not act on them. Acknowledge them yes, but do not let them make you behave in ways harmful to yourself. Do not say loving words or do loving things for your partner after he has mistreated you. Don't be nice to him, even if you feel it. Remove yourself from his presence, even if you do not want to.

Deny yourself the feeling of pleasure of letting anyone come into your life to demean you in any way. Don't reinforce the feelings that are causing you to behave in self-destructive ways by exposing yourself to the things or people that trigger them off. If you don't want violence in your life, don't watch it on television, don't read about, think about it, talk about or associate with violent people. Are you afraid? Don't feed that feeling by thinking about it. Never acknowledge it. If there is danger because your reasoning has told you it is there, do what you have to do to remove yourself or the person that is the cause. Think it out and act on it, but do not feed the feeling of fear. Command yourself in a kind way not to act on it. Do you feel sorry for your abuser after he apologizes to you for hurting you? Reason it out. Is it genuine? Is feeling sorry for the enemy appropriate? If you have trouble figuring it out, give yourself six months to think about it. Then let him know whether you accept his apology or not. In the meantime, of course, don't feed the feeling by seeing him or talking to him. Make it simple. Don't complicate it. You don't want to feel nervous? Get rid of the thing that is making you nervous. You don't want to be sworn at or humiliated? Remove yourself from the person who is doing it to you. Don't want any scratches or bruises on your body? Don't want to be hit? Stay out of the way of the fist. For any kind of feeling that stems from programming and is harmful to you, do not talk about, think about it, expose yourself to the things that trigger it off, do not even try to analyze it. (You can explore these feelings in therapy if you wish when it is feasible. However, I found it unwise to do so while I was trying to create a new reality on my own, day to day) That is what is meant by not reinforcing a feeling. When a feeling is not fed by the mind and given energy, it diminishes. That is how it grew in the first place, it was fed by your thinking process until it became second nature to you. Your buttons were constantly pushed, the feeling was continually reinforced. If you want a feeling to grow, such as the warm feeling you get when you are loved by a truly loving man, nurture it. Read about it. Concentrate on it, daydream about it. Watch movies and be around couples who are joyously in love. You will eventually manifest this for yourself exactly the same way you created an abusive relationship in the past. This time though, you will be conscious of the process and you will have control over it. You can pick and choose what you want rather than be pulled towards a certain individual for no apparent reason. It won't be a mysterious, perplexing thing.

When you do this, by the way, your programmed destructive feelings aren't going to like it one bit. They're going to come back and back. Even though you do not act on them, you will still have the feelings. For example, perhaps you are in situation where you have left your partner and are experiencing feelings of loneliness and desire. It's not hard to get your emotions to correspond to the facts. Just visualize the times he hurt, demeaned and attacked you. Re-live it vividly in your mind. Or do as I did, get out a tape recording of some of the verbal abuse incidents you experienced with him and listen to it. (I did this deliberately for this purpose at the time I was involved with my partner) Or call someone who is close to you and start talking about all the miserable things you experienced with him. Soon enough you will find your feelings changing. You will probably become angry and greatly relieved you are away from him. Pat yourself on the back. You didn't give in to the feeling of desire by contacting him, you reasoned it out and acknowledged the reality of him, and you responded appropriately to this reality by experiencing anger and relief. In time this procedure will become automatic.

Or, try this: put someone you admire, such as an actress, or a person you love in your own situation. It might be Goldie Hawn or Linda Evans. See her in your movie, your life. See her with the man you love. Have her act out the scenes just as you do. It will make you gasp. You will find yourself telling her, no, don't do that! Can't you see what he is doing? He's lying to you! He's cruel! Run! Get away from him, it's dangerous! Why are you with him? You're so beautiful, how can you lower yourself like this? Now you are starting to sound like the outsiders looking in, except for one difference: you are on your own side, not against yourself.

Of course, "programming" is not the only cause of feelings that clash with reality. From time to time you may also experience the "psychic" part of yourself that warns you of danger or enables you to foresee events in the future without apparent logical cause. This is a manifestation of your natural, loving self. It is vital to learn the difference between this intuitive, natural element of your consciousness and those programmed responses which can be so harmful. To learn more about this read *Real Magic* by Dr. Wayne W. Dyer (Harper, 1992).

You will discover that when you use your natural gifts life is truly worth living.

Without knowledge, you are powerless. With it you can create any reality you desire. It is priceless.

Chapter 4

Knowledge is Power

Because so many women search for and ask about books on the subject of abuse, it is imperative that they find them. Books can save lives, our self-esteem and our sanity. They can give us the knowledge we need to help ourselves.

One of the earliest, and, I believe, one of the best books ever written about battered women is *The Battered Woman* by Lenore Walker. (Harper & Row, 1979) She began studying the problem in 1975 when "no other psychologists were doing similar research," and found that domestic violence towards women was a disturbing problem of greater proportions than anyone imagined. She, along with others, estimated that as many as 50 percent of all women will be battering victims at some point in their lives. Walker defined the term "battered woman" as "a woman who is repeatedly subjected to any forceful physical or psychological behavior by a man in order to coerce her to do something he wants her to do without any concerns for her rights." Today her book is considered a classic and it is doubtful that there is one shelter for battered women in this country that does not keep one treasured copy of it to pass around as recommended reading.

Del Martin's *Battered Wives* (Simon & Schuster, 1976) was published just before Lenore Walker's book and it also received wide attention. According to Diane Russell, who at that time was coordinator of the U.S. Delegation to the International Tribunal on Crimes Against

Please Don't Let Him Hurt Me Anymore

Women, "Martin admits that it is impossible to know the exact prevalence of wife-beating and battery in this country because no satisfactory large-scale prevalence study has been undertaken to date...she makes it clear that we know enough to realize that there is an enormous problem which is being ignored. With the publication of this book, the continued neglect of this problem will be inexcusable."

Battered Wives encompasses concerns such as legislation, financial aid and survival tactics as well as the social forces that keep women in violent relationships. Though books remain among the most powerful indicators of current trends and values in our country,we need to ask if this book and the many excellent works on this subject published in the last twenty years (many listed on the following pages) have compelled us to cease our neglect of marital violence and change our legislation and attitudes? Has the phenomenal *Women Who Love Too Much* (Simon & Schuster, 1985) prompted social enlightenment? What about the startling book *The Verbally Abusive Relationship?* Has the new light it sheds on the complexities of verbal abuse caused society to take a new look at how we can preserve family units by learning how to communicate without inflicting pain on each other. Did *The Burning Bed* (Harcourt Brace Jovanovich, 1980) by Faith McNulty, which was made into one of the most watched television movies ever, cause us to become so outraged that we demanded the violence against women *must* stop? No, these books have not succeeded in dispelling inexcusable neglect of an issue that is hell bent on destroying the very foundation of society. More women today are murdered by their partners than in the past. Health and Human Services Secretary Donna Shalala stated that domestic violence is an unacknowledged epidemic in our country. Why should it take Nicole Brown

Simpson's murder in June, 1994, and subsequent revelations of the abuse she suffered at the hands of her celebrity husband, to heighten society's awareness and cause lawmakers to scramble to pass bills that mandate arrest for those who commit a domestic assault? Why should it take the national airing of Nicole Simpson's taped 1993 911 call to police for help while her husband O.J. Simpson ranted, raved and threatened in the background to cause the whole nation to finally sit up and look domestic violence straight in the eye? A look yes, not necessarily a supportive one in many instances. Receiving letters in prison at the rate of 3500 per day in Los Angeles, O.J. Simpson, charged with the murder of his wife and her male companion, has already been excused by many supporters for his violent acts against Nicole. As one male supporter blatantly put it, "I don't care what he's done. I still like him."

What books about spousal abuse have done is educated, supported, informed, encouraged and outraged millions of women in their personal lives. We have been able to connect to each other through these publications, knowing we are not alone. They have given us the courage to come forward and seek help. They have brought us to our knees and caused us to weep in pain, knowing horrifying acts committed against us cannot be humanely tolerated. We've come to understand ourselves and each other and we now have a semblance of what to do, where to go, and we can see a light at the end of the tunnel.

Books are like friends. They speak to us in our quiet moments, our dark desperate times and are always there for us to refer to. When nothing else is available, when no one comes to our aid, there is a book that does. We are grateful to the authors of these books, for the time, courage, energy and struggle it took to write them. Grateful too that there were publishers who published them. Gone are the days when to find one of these books in a bookstore was a major accomplishment. Today we have many of them. For every question, every need we have concerning pain or problems in our relationships with men, there is a friend to be found on paper.

Though the best places to find these publications are in women's bookstores, they can also be found in other independent bookstores and in the major chain bookstores. Your best bet in the long run, however, will always be women's bookstores. They're up to date, knowledgeable and will go to great lengths to help you find a book. They can order a publication for you, mail it to you or tuck it under the counter until you can pick it up.

Women's bookstores are fascinating resources as well. Everything from feminist newspapers to brochures and business cards can be found in them. And at the really good ones... you can sit and have a cup of tea.

Where would we be without them?

Recommended Reading

CHILDREN IN THE CROSSFIRE
Violence In The Home ...
How Does It Affect Our Children?
Roy (Health Communications, 1988)

This book answers the question: To what extent does living in a home where Mom is battered and beaten by Dad affect a child's self-esteem, future choices of a spouse, destructive coping mechanisms, etc.? The legal, social, history of spousal, child abuse and their interconnectedness is explored.

THE ONES WHO GOT AWAY
Women Who Left Abusive Partners
NiCarthy (Seal Press - Feminist, 1987)

Interviews over 30 women.

CALLED TO ACCOUNT
Switzer (Seal Press - Feminist, 1987)

Harrowing account of how she helped her husband change his battering behavior.

BATTERED WIVES
Updated edition
Del Martin (Simon & Schuster, 1976)

Updated classic on the psychology and politics of domestic violence.

TALKING IT OUT
A Guide To Groups For Abused Women
NiCarthy (Seal Press - Feminist, 1989)

A handbook for starting and sustaining a group for battered women.

NAMING THE VIOLENCE
Speaking Out About Lesbian Battering
Lobel (Seal Press - Feminist, 1986)

Anthology.

DOMESTIC VIOLENCE ON TRIAL
Sonki (Springer Publishing Co., Inc., 1987)

Legal and psychological aspects of battering, court procedures and child custody.

THE BATTERED WOMAN
Walker (Harper & Row, 1979)

The three-stage cycle of battering and avenues of help.

GETTING FREE
A Handbook For Women In Abusive Relationships
(Second edition)
NiCarthy (Seal Press - Feminist, 1986)

Self-help resource for abused women, including lesbian abuse and teen abuse.

YOU CAN BE FREE
An Easy To Read Handbook for Abused Women
NiCarthy (Seal Press - Feminist, 1989)

A simplified version of *Getting Free*.

AGAINST OUR WILL
Brownmiller (Bantam Books, 1981)

Possibly the definitive work on the social, economic and political history of rape and society's complicity in keeping women in their place... at home behind closed doors.

HEROES OF THEIR OWN LIVES
The Politics and History of Family Violence...
Boston 1880-1960
Gordon (Penguin, U.S.A., 1989)

A historical investigation of child abuse, child neglect, wife-beating and incest. Poignant case studies speak for themselves.

MEJOR SOLA QUE MAL ACOMPAÑADA
FOR THE LATINA IN AN ABUSIVE RELATIONSHIP
Zambrano (Seal Press - Feminist, 1985)

Bilingual edition. Excellent resource that covers everything: identifying the abuse, dealing with your religious beliefs, and getting your fair share of the property settlements.

CHAIN, CHAIN, CHANGE
For Black Women Dealing With
Physical and Emotional Abuse
White (Seal Press - Feminist, 1985)

Sexism and racism are intertwined in the abuse of women, and when it is culturally sanctioned, it may feel like there is no escape. Whether you are a Black woman with a man, or a Black lesbian, this book is a must.

GROWING BEYOND ABUSE
A Workbook for Survivors of Sexual Exploitation
or Childhood Sexual Abuse
Nestinger and Lewis (Omni Recovery, Inc., 1991)

For those who wish to achieve greater insight, awareness and growth. Includes poetry and exercises. Beautiful, therapeutic and could change your life.

AWAKENING YOUR SEXUALITY
A Recovery Guide for Women
Covington (Harper, San Francisco, 1992)

Honest and courageous. Important information for women. Moving and compassionate.

WOMEN AND MALE VIOLENCE
The Visions and Struggles
of the Battered Women's Movement
Schechter (South End Press, 1982)

An in-depth look at abuse and society's attitudes. Comprehensive. Describes the Battered Women's Movement and its history. An important and compassionate book.

MEN'S WORK
How to Stop the Violence That Tears Our Lives Apart
Kivel (Ballantine, 1992)

Written by Paul Kivel, the founder of the Oakland Men's Project, this is one of the few books that speaks about men's violence towards women from a man's point of view. Describes how men learn violence and how to stop it.

MEN WHO CAN'T LOVE
How to Recognize a Commitment-phobic Man
Before He Breaks Your Heart
Carter and Sokol (Berkley Publishing Group, 1987)

Excellent read to help understand why some men do not want to commit. Advice on how to leave and find someone who will stay and has the ability to love. Not specifically for women in abusive relationships, but brings up many of the same problems.

NEXT TIME, SHE'LL BE DEAD
Battering and How to Stop It
Jones (Beacon Press, 1994)

A revealing, sobering look at the attitudes and institutions which foster the problem of violence against women. Here's a book that finally comes uo with some answers. Tremendous in its understanding.

THE BURNING BED
McNulty (Harcourt, Brace, Jovanovich, 1980)

True story of Faith McNulty who was portrayed by Farrah Fawcett on one of television's most watched movies. Tells her story in her own words and is one of the very first books published about what it is like to be a battered woman. Both horrifying and insightful. A classic.

SHATTERED DREAMS
Fedders and Elliott (Dell Publishing, 1987)

A true story of the wife of a prominent lawyer in the Reagan government. She endured physical and emotional abuse for seventeen years before she broke free. Very helpful in understanding the process of getting free.

THE BATTERED WOMAN'S SURVIVAL GUIDE
Statman (Taylor Publishing, 1992)

A guide to breaking the cycle of violence and a listing of general resources. Real life case histories, a detailed profile of the man who abuses, legal help and how to help a woman who doesn't ask for it. Recommended for victims as well as relatives, friends and professionals.

WOMEN WHO LOVE TOO MUCH
Norwood (Simon & Schuster, 1985)

One of the most important books ever written to help women in abusive relationships. Delves deeply into the reasons women love men who cannot love them in return. Explicit guidance on how to break the addiction and heal.

LETTERS FROM WOMEN WHO LOVE TOO MUCH
Norwood (Pocket Books, 1988)

The follow-up book to Women Who Love Too Much. Insight into the real lives of the readers who read the first book, with emphasis on putting her principles of recovery into practice.

MEN WHO HATE WOMEN AND
THE WOMEN WHO LOVE THEM
Forward (Bantam, 1987)

One of the most well-known books on the subject of women in abusive relationships. A self-help guide, Dr. Forward helps you to understand your man's destructive behavior, the pattern, the part you play in it, how to break the pattern, heal the hurt and gain your self-respect.

THE WAY UP FROM DOWN
Slagle (St. Martin's Press, 1987)

When a woman experiences a crisis, the first thing that deteriorates is her physical health. In this informative self-help book, the author promotes a safe and easy program of vitamins and amino acids to relieve depression and fatigue.

An interesting and vital read.

THE WAR AGAINST WOMEN
French (Simon & Schuster, 1992)

French, the best-selling author of *The Women's Room,* shows in this controversial book that women are regarded in a negative light the world over. Through research, she shows the "economic, political and physical suppression and abuse of women and children everywhere." Shocking. Convincing and upsetting.

THE VERBALLY ABUSIVE RELATIONSHIP
How to Recognize It and Respond
Evans (Bob Adams, 1992)

How to identify and handle a verbally abusive partner. Tremendous book in the strides it takes. Unusual clarity in descriptions and how-to steps. The first of its kind. The author is exceptional in understanding and insight.

MARRYING THE HANGMAN
Weller (Random House, 1991)

True story about a young woman who was murdered by her husband. Clearly reports that wealth, privilege and intelligence do not protect one from abuse. Chilling.

THE EMOTIONALLY ABUSED WOMAN
Overcoming Destructive Patterns
 and Reclaiming Yourself
Engel (Ballantine Books, 1990)

A compassionate therapist, Engel offers the reader a guide to self exploration and recovery. Delves into childhood and patterns. Author has been there.

ABUSED NO MORE
Recovery for Women from Abusive
or Co-dependent Relationships
Ackerman and Pickering (TAB Books, 1989)

Practical and helpful. How to recognize abuse and get out of the trap. Easy to understand.

WHEN LOVE GOES WRONG
Strategies for Women with Controlling Partners
Jones and Schechter (Harper Collins, 1993)

Full of practical advice and insight. Covers everything from why to how. Honest and up-to-date. Leaves no questions unanswered. Authors are very experienced and knowledgeable.

LOVESICK
Why Women Become Addicted To The Wrong Men and What To Do About It
Macavoy and Isrealson (Donald I. Fine, Inc., 1991)

Based on the belief that women who don't love themselves sabotage their love lives, this book provides self awareness, insights and recovery tips. Sincere and emotional.

ARMED AND FEMALE
Quigley (St. Martin's, 1993)

For the woman who chooses to arm herself or explore the possibility of protecting herself through the use of a gun. Says Cybill Shepherd on the back of her book, "To paraphrase Elizabeth Cady Stanton, until more women learn to use the weapons of men to defend themselves, they will continue to be victims of men..." A book by a woman for women. Includes listings of the laws in all states and such things as registration, permits, ownership and shooting stances. An important read.

BOOK 11: HOW TO GET ANYTHING ON ANYBODY
The Encyclopedia of Personal Surveillance
Lapin (ISECO, Inc., 1991)

BEING SAFE
Mandell (Doubleday, 1978)

Covers everything from common sense to security systems. Explores guard dogs, products and services. A reliable reference. Book may only be available in libraries.

BEGINNING TO HEAL
The First Book for Survivors of Child Sexual Abuse
Bass and Davis (Harper Collins, 1994)

An introduction to the healing process for all women. Based on the national bestseller, T*he Courage to Heal.*

FROM PAYCHECK TO POWER
The Working Woman's Guide to Reducing Debt,
Building Assets and Getting What You Want Out Of Life
Bessette and Wilson (August House, 1992)

Addresses the emotional aspect of handling money and offers a guide to reducing debt and building assets. Teaches you to manage your money and not live by old messages such as, "girls will be taken care of," and "as a woman, you put your own needs last."

Please Don't Let Him Hurt Me Anymore

HEALING YOUR LIFE
Recovery From Domestic Violence
Henekens (ProWriting Services and Press, 1991)

Available in bookstores as well as by mail. Send $8.95 plus $2 postage and handling to: PS & P ProWriting Services and Press, P.O. Box 383, Fallcreek, WI, 54742 or call (715) 877-2303.

WOMEN'S ENCYCLOPEDIA OF HEALTH
& EMOTIONAL HEALING
Top Doctors Share Their Unique Self-Help Advice
On Your Body, Your Feelings and Your Life
Nechas and Wallis (Rodale Press, 1992)

For women, by women. Covers the leading physical and emotional concerns of women today. For all ages. Warm and understanding. Helps you to help yourself.

Chapter 5

Hospitals, Emergencies and Medical Aid

Dr. Kevin Fullin, a 36-year-old AMA (American Medical Association member) from Kenosha, Wisconsin, states, "A third of all women's injuries coming into our emergency rooms are no accidents. Most are the result of deliberate, premeditated acts of violence. And frequently they occur over and over until the woman is killed."

"Family violence is one of America's most critical health issues," continues Dr. Fullin. "Yet society repeatedly sweeps it under the rug. There's a tendency to rationalize this as a personal problem they should settle themselves. And tragically, the victim returns home to be beaten again."

Wisconsin's first Domestic Violence Advocate Program was created by this concerned physician, along with doctors and administrators sharing his determination.

"We learned that these women were shielding the person who was beating them to protect themselves and their children," says Dr. Fullin. "But now our advocates can identify with these women as victims and remove them from the cycle of violence."

Inspired by this physician's bold community program, the American Medical Association created The Physicians' Campaign Against Family Violence designed to address the problem on a national level.

Recognizing that doctors are the first to see abused patients in hospital emergency rooms, they published a set of guidelines to help physicians identify this as criminal abuse. What this means for a woman who ends up in emergency because of severe physical damage inflicted upon her by her partner, is that she will no longer be treated just for her injuries, but as a whole person with a problem. She will be offered intervention counseling and options, no longer just patched up and sent home. She will be understood and treated with sympathy. There are over 300,000 AMA physicians familiar with these guidelines in the country, but unfortunately not every hospital will have one or enough of them.

For women who are in dangerous situations, it is advisable to find a physician who is sympathetic and knowledgeable in the area of abuse before anything traumatic happens to her. In that way, if she is hurt and has to go to emergency, she can call her doctor and receive the support she needs. She will be acknowledged regarding the violence in her life; the fact that violence is illegal will be communicated to her; she will be assured that it's not her fault; the police will be called for her; and arrangements will be made for her to go to a safe place.

With more and more physicians becoming informed and supportive, abused women will no longer be afraid to go to hospitals when necessary. Instead of being treated as outcasts, they will be treated with dignity and compassion.

Choosing Your Physician Wisely

Before you begin your search, ask yourself a question: what kind of physician do I want? Do I want a family practitioner; a pediatrician or obstetrician; an internist who practices family medicine; another type of specialist.

You may want to begin by finding a primary care physician who you like and trust. Your primary care physician can then help you choose specialists when necessary. After you've decided what direction you want to go in, you'll want the names of physicians who can meet your needs.

There are several sources of information about physicians available. First, you can contact your local (county) or state medical society. These groups often have referral services and can offer advice on hospitals and health care programs in your area. A second source is friends and relatives. Finally, referral services sponsored by hospitals and other providers may be available.

If you belong to a Health Maintenance Organization (HMO), Preferred Provider Organization (PPO), or other employer health insurance plan, it may affect the choices you have, since the group may have a list of physicians from which to choose. Although you may have to choose one of the physicians in the group, the group assists you by pre-screening its physicians' credentials.

Once you have the names of several physicians, learn as much about them as you can. You'll want to know what their credentials and qualifications are. Some of this information can be obtained, again, from your local or state medical society or the AMA's American Medical Directory, available at most libraries. Most physicians and their staffs will be happy to answer your questions.

Here are some of the more important questions to ask:

- What hospitals are you affiliated with?

  It is important to know in advance the hospitals your physician is affiliated with so there are no surprises in a medical emergency. Location may be important to you, too, for ease of access or availability of close family support.

- What is your fee schedule? How do you accept payment and when should it be made?

Physicians should discuss and explain their fees and billing practices to you. Some physicians even post their fees for the most common services in their office. Talk to your physician about how fees are determined.

- Do you accept Medicare? (If applicable)

If the answer is "Yes," find out if the physician will accept what Medicare pays as full payment. This is known as "accepting assignment." Many physicians have formal participation agreements with Medicare, and accept assignment in all cases. Many physicians do not participate but still see Medicare patients and accept assignment on a case-by-case basis.

- How would you feel about my obtaining a second opinion on your diagnosis or recommended therapies?

When thinking about serious non-emergency medical care, it is not uncommon to seek the advice of another qualified physician. There may be differences of opinion. If the two disagree, most people find they have the facts they need to make their own decision.

- How can I contact you if an emergency arises when your office is closed?

Make sure you know what your physician's policy is in an emergency and clearly understand how it works. Can you contact the physician directly day or night? What about weekends and holidays? What arrangements are made when the physician is away on business or vacation?

- Do you believe that whatever a patient tells you is confidential?

Patient-physician privilege is a long-standing time-honored tradition in the medical profession. However, there may be times when a physician is required to release information to the state and federal government—for example, an outbreak of measles.

• Do you always get patient permission before releasing records?

A physician normally will not release your records unless you have already given general consent, such as when: you want another physician to look at your records; your primary care physician is consulting another physician; your insurance company has requested it; you are checking into a clinic or hospital; you have a medical emergency.

• What would you want to know about me, other than my medical history and current health?

Your physician should want to know as much about you as possible. This includes your attitude, your state of mind, even intimate details about your personal life. Do not be surprised or embarrassed when the physician asks you whether you drink or smoke, how your marriage is, how your children are, if you are happy at your job, and if your sex life is okay. This is normal and these are important to your overall well-being.

Domestic Violence:
No Longer A Family Secret

The American home is more dangerous to women than city streets. Every 15 seconds a woman is battered in America.

Every five years, domestic violence kills as many

women as the total number of Americans who died in the Vietnam War.

And domestic violence is the single largest cause of injury to women in the United States—more common than injuries sustained from car accidents, muggings and rapes combined.

Every year, domestic violence results in almost 100,000 days of hospitalization, almost 30,000 emergency department visits and almost 40,000 visits to a physician. Thirty-five percent of women who seek treatment at hospital emergency rooms are there for symptoms of ongoing abuse. (Note: Many women do not seek medical help when they should, so there is no way of knowing exact numbers.)

Perhaps the most disturbing are the ongoing patterns of domestic abuse. Children who are abused—or see abuse in the home—often establish violent and abusive homes when they are adults, passing the brutal pattern of behavior to their children.

The American Medical Association believes family violence is a disease, not simply a problem for the courts and legal system.

If you are a victim of domestic abuse, *seek help*.

(Adapted from information provided by the
American Medical Association, with permission)

Many women, out of fear or shame, do not go to a hospital emergency room or see a physician when injured. Some injuries cannot be self-treated, and medical care is vital. The following conditions should receive immediate medical attention:

Lacerations
If a severe cut or wound is not stitched together within 24 hours, it may become dangerously infected and the doctor will not be able to stitch it back together.

Fractured Bones

These need immediate attention since they can be life-threatening injuries. Call an ambulance.

Severe Emotional Pain

Do not be afraid to get help in this instance. A physician can do much to help alleviate major emotional stress such as fear and anxiety.

Losing Consciousness

Fainting may be an indication of a serious problem, especially during pregnancy or after being physically assaulted. An examination is vital.

Calling 911

When calling 911 to get help for your injuries, follow these steps:

- Give your telephone number first, then your address

- Describe your condition (or those of any other injured person) i.e. possible broken bone, pain in your abdomen, bleeding from a wound in your head.

- Tell the operator how the injury happened, if there is anyone else in the house who needs help or if you are still in a threatening situation (where you could be injured further)

- Give the operator your name

- Stay on the line, do not hang up until help arrives. Emergency personnel might want to ask you additional questions or may be able to advise you about immediate methods to treat your injuries.

WHAT DO YOU DO?
WHERE DO YOU GO?

Where do you go when you're alone?
You're world has split apart
And you don't know who to telephone
Or where to start

What do you do when your friends and family
Tell you they'd help you if they could
But they just can't understand your reality?
You keep looking for an outstretched hand
To grasp and lead the way
And pray to God
You make it through one more day

Chapter 6

What Is A Shelter and Where Can I Find One?

Shelters are places of safety and confidentiality for women who are in danger of being physically or mentally harmed by their abusive partners. They are usually a last resort, and, typically, are not advertised. Most often a woman is referred to a shelter by a doctor, a hospital, a police officer or a counselor. Varying in size, location and policies, all of them offer counseling programs, resources and referrals. Food, clothing and other necessities are normally supplied. Children are welcome and all shelters provide toys, clothing and educational programs for them. Pets are generally not allowed (though the odd one has made its way into a house now and then for various outrageous reasons) and no visitors are allowed in most of them.

Because a woman's arrival at a shelter is usually preceded by a period of trauma and shock, a great deal of her time will be spent in counseling and support groups. By reputation, the quality of therapy available in some shelters is unsurpassed.

Lives have been salvaged, saved and patched up in these havens and we need more of them. We also need to let more women know they exist. It is a sad fact that abuse in our society is a much larger problem than statistics admit and, unfortunately, there are not enough shelters to accommodate the many women who need them. Recent legislative activity, fortunately, promises to add to their numbers, but more will still be needed.

Information and Facts
You Should Know About Shelters

- Space is limited. For every one accepted, two are turned away. Five to seven women are left without shelter for every 2 women served in urban areas (National Coalition Against Domestic Violence).

- Shelters have different criteria for accepting women.

  Some will *not* accept you if you:

  - Are single
  - Are on prescribed "mood altering" medication such as anti-depressants
  - Do not have a police report
  - Are an active alcoholic or addicted to drugs
  - Call on weekends or if the director is not available
  - Are out of their area (county)
  - Are not calling from an emergency room or police station
  - Have not been physically abused
  - Have been in the shelter once before

- Some shelters have a seven day probation period, others three days. Some require that you do not make outside calls for the first three days.

- Not all personnel or volunteers answering a crisis line are well-informed nor always particularly sympathetic to you or your plight. Most of them are, but not all, so do not be afraid to challenge them if you feel they are not informing you properly or giving you enough attention.

Some Common Questions

What do I do when I call?

Be very definite that you need to be in a shelter and tell them why. If they tell you they will call you back, wait. They will. If you feel anxious and cannot wait, call them back. Try to stay calm. Answer all their questions to the best of your ability. If you can't speak, get someone else to do it for you (if there is someone).

How do I get there?

If you do not have your own car, tell them. They can usually make arrangements to have you driven by taxi. If there is a friend or relative who can drive you, ask them. You will not be given the address of the shelter, but of their office and from there you will be taken to the shelter by staff.

What should I bring?

Money... personal belongings... valuables... important papers. (Only if you have time.) Do not bring blankets, towels, sheets, dishes, utensils, pans, pieces of furniture or the like unless you are particularly attached to them. Radios, alarm clocks and can openers seem to be in short supply at some shelters, so bring them if you can. (Most women only grab a suitcase and their children—others sometimes have a bit of time to prepare—it depends on the situation.)

What does it look like?

Some shelters look like a plain house, others like a motel with individual apartments. Some have separate cottages. In almost all of them, women and children double up and share either a room or an apartment-type unit. Everything needed for cooking, bathing, laundry and quiet time is provided.

What about my children?

Most shelters try hard to provide what facilities they can for children. Playrooms, playgrounds, toys and equipment, classes and children's movies are not uncommon. Children are very precious and are given every consideration. They truly are innocent victims of domestic violence.

Will they help me establish a new life?

Yes. They will do what they can. Everyone is assigned an advocate and practical matters such as obtaining funds, housing, medical care, restraining orders, food, clothing, furniture and job opportunities are all dealt with.

How will I feel?

Many women experience depression and fear at first. The are also often overwhelmed by the amount of strength that is required (not to mention courage) to break away from their old life and begin anew. One of the greatest comforts they find is in each other. They share a common bond and many new friendships are formed. Slowly, with each step, they begin to feel better.

Dana's Stay: A Personal Account

It took everything I had to leave the relationship I was in, checking into a motel first, then a shelter the next day. The reason I was accepted was because I had already attended the outreach program the shelter provided for women who were still living with their abusive men so they knew me. I didn't want to go. Everything I owned was left behind, I had to put my precious feline friend into a strange boarding place and I knew I was going to have a struggle to get a place of my own to live. With very little money, no real friends and in a very depressed state, I was close to committing suicide. "Why did he have to do this to me?" I screamed inwardly in anguish. We could have had a good life but he wouldn't stop. Day after day, the screaming, the insults, the pushing, shoving and choking. Trying to squeeze the life out of me. Well, he had succeeded. I didn't have much life left in me. Haggard, thin and storing a deep hopelessness within, I felt too weak to go on.

As soon as I saw the shelter I wanted to run. I balked at the sight in front of me. A wooden gate, high and old with the paint peeling off, beckoned to me. It couldn't be much better inside, I muttered to myself. Oh God, I felt like crying. I just stood there looking at it, clutching a strong box and a suitcase. This was going to be a far cry from the lovely middle class home I had run away from. I felt homesick. For him, the house, my bed, the yard, my belongings. I made myself follow the intake worker inside. Sure enough, it was worse than I thought. A row of motel-like apartments formed a square bleakly enveloping what appeared to be a playground in the middle with an assortment of well used patio furniture and kids playthings—a slide, a sandbox and toys. A few women and children were quietly sitting around and smiled at me as I made my way to the office. I handed over my strong box for safe keeping, was given a bag of groceries and filled out forms agreeing to their general rules and regulations. A few hugs by warm staff members and then I was escorted to my "apartment" which I would share with two other women, African-American, slightly younger than I, in their middle thirties. I, being Caucasian, had very little knowledge or experience with relationships with women not of my race, but they were both so friendly, I took to them immediately. They helped me unpack my things and settle into the small, aged, but clean haven where I would be for the next thirty days.

The first day was the hardest. The night was worse, hot and long. I couldn't sleep. I kept hearing cries and moans. Children would softly whimper and a steady drone of whispers seemed to continue into the early hours of the morning. The next day I began to assess the company I was in. Talking to the women that were there, it did not take long for me to feel intense compassion and comradeship with them. In many ways, they were so much like me. Though our ethnic and economic backgrounds varied, our psychological and physical bruises were the same. Because of this it was easy to form a bond.

I was most affected by my roommate Rachel who had arrived just hours before me. Tall, lanky, beautiful, her delicate face harbored the most haunting eyes I had ever seen. It was no wonder. I later discovered she had fled her home after her husband had knocked her unconscious. She woke up on the floor, dazed, terrified, crawling on her hands and knees to get out of the house through the kitchen door so he wouldn't see her. He was still watching television. The fear of death lingered in her eyes for a long time. She still had it before I left the shelter. I had never seen this before in my life. Maybe I too, had that look. Rachel's finely chiseled face bore knife scars from years ago. She had been with her abuser for almost 20 years and had endured many tormenting rituals such as "Russian roulette" and listening to his plans of how he was going to kill her, how they would never find him. It was Rachel who made me cry when I heard her speak softly to me in the dark of our apartment, "You know, no one <u>really</u> cares about battered women. Not really." That was all she said and it hung in the air like a truth that would eventually be realized in my own life. It wasn't true for all women. It was for Rachel and it was for me for quite some time, until I found those in the world that did care, could care.

Every evening we had group sessions. We shared our suffering, memories and denial. It was all the same, The terror. The desperation. The confusion of "Was it my fault?" The wrenching question "Why?" stayed on all our lips and never quite seemed to be answered. We were all different, yet all the same. We all knew how to run, how to hide. We all knew the pain of physical abuse. We all felt ashamed, humiliated. We survived what seemed impossible to survive. Battered beaten, betrayed.

Daylight found most of us either in private therapy sessions or going out beyond the old gate into the world to find a new place to live, a job or money. With the help of sympathetic and supportive staff, many of us formed workable plans to get ourselves back on our feet. There were those of us who weren't strong enough and went back to the ones who were hurting them. "No, don't go," the rest of us would plead with them, to no avail. After all, we had all done the same thing at one time or another. Left and gone back, not able to build a support system "out there" to carry us, protect us, hold us up. We understood.

For myself, I managed to get a loan from the shelter to get an apartment and arrange an income from independent work in sales. It was just as hard leaving as it was to walk in that first day. I no longer saw the shabbiness of the place. My only focus was the women I was leaving behind. I looked at them and their children. What would happen to them? Would they make it. Knowing them as I had, I knew some of them would not be safe out in the world. They would have a difficult time. It was agonizing. Some of them would die.

I eventually found caring, loving people out in the world. I healed. I learned. It was never easy. But I did it. And of course, I found work helping battered women. How could I not? What I saw while I was in the shelter, I could not forget. I do not think anyone who experienced what I did could just walk away and forget and not help.

I feel very strange out in the world, though. I find so many people insensitive to the plight of battered women. They are unwilling to help or to understand. Domestic violence is not on the "hot list" for charities or

Please Don't Let Him Hurt Me Anymore

private donations. It is a topic most often avoided. Worse than that, it often brings out the worst in people. Stone silence. Condemnation. Jokes. Refusal to help when they so easily can.

I do not understand what this is, this coldness, this cruelty. I do not understand this rage men have against women. Most of us are peaceful and loving. Yes, I have studied and analyzed all the reasons why men batter women. I know about conditioning. I have the answers in words. Yet, in some strange way I can't explain, I don't really understand it. I don't emotionally grasp why men hate women.

You know, that old shelter is still standing today, sheltering woman after woman. I drove by it the other day. I've never told a soul of it's location. My eyes filled with tears.

I'm out here now. I've made it. I will help, do all I can to teach and stand up for women's peace and safety. And one of these fine days these old havens will be standing empty.

We'll live in a world where we are all at home...safe.

Chapter 7

Housing and Relocating

One of the most anxiety-provoking questions you'll ever ask yourself is, "Where will I live?" Especially if you have a low income or none at all. It runs a close second to, "What will I do with the kids?"

Housing for women with children on a low income such as welfare is basically non-existent. I have witnessed women attempting to find an apartment on the money welfare provides, and, yes, they do exist, but in the slums. What is the answer?

Money.

If you have financial resources, finding a safe, secure abode is not hard to do. The thing here is to make sure your abuser does not find you. There are ways to ensure this, and it is best to talk to a therapist or people in your support group who are knowledgeable in this area. Security systems, body guards, restraining orders, unlisted telephone numbers, obtaining a post office box for your mail and putting your water and power under another name are just some of the things that can be done to protect your home from being located. Many women have been outraged at having to move from apartment to apartment to avoid being harassed by their former mates. They are beginning to stand up and question why they should be living like fugitives. It is a wrenching question. Why should they? In extreme cases of violence, some women feel the only alternative is to get a gun and shoot the batterer. Fortunately, most women are very level headed and do manage to conceal there whereabouts.

If you should decide to rent an apartment instead of a house, there are some things you should keep in mind. Make sure you pick a neighborhood that is not too far from your work or the schools you or your kids need to attend. Another factor in choosing an area is the kind of people that live there. For example some areas are dominated by singles under 34 years of age whereas other places are populated by those in retirement. Try to find out as much information as you can before making a commitment to a particular neighborhood. Is it relatively safe? Quiet? Is the air quality good or is it smoggy? It is a good idea to call a licensed rental listing service or a real estate agency. They will be able to guide you when choosing a neighborhood.

When making your decision which apartment to rent, look for a building that is in good condition on the outside and has well kept grounds. Check for outside lighting in walkways and where you would park your car. Inside, check for locks and smoke detectors as well as who your neighbor will be and health hazards such as insects. Is it well ventilated? Does it have good air circulation? Does everything work? Appliances, air conditioning and plumbing could be faulty. Does the place *feel* good? Are you comfortable?

Most landlords, of course, are concerned about your ability to pay and your personality. Be prepared with references from your previous apartment and have proof of your ability to pay the rent. Your income should be at least three times that of the price of the rent per month. If you decide to sign a lease, be careful of the terms and your rights should you have to terminate it. Also, be sure of the laws in your state regarding security deposits. Too many times landlords try to get out of returning security deposits and you may end up suing in small claims court.

If you do not have a suitable income to rent a house or an apartment in a safe neighborhood, it would be wise to investigate sharing a home with someone else. You can find agencies that specialize in locating suitable house mates, including those with children. Such arrangements can work out very well. There are many ways this is beneficial for you. It is much safer to live with someone else than be alone, especially if you are afraid your abuser might still find you. Perhaps a new-found friend who has been in a similar abusive situation would like to find a house to rent with you. The two of you could help each other in the respect that, as former battered women, you are familiar with each other's safety concerns. If you are single, you might consider renting a room with a compatible family. Expect to pay more for a private bath and entrance. These situations can work out wonderfully for those who cannot afford to pay for a separate dwelling of their own. It should be stressed however, that you should feel comfortable in the home or room you choose. You do not need the anxiety of having to cope with house mates who are not compatible. After leaving an abusive relationship, you will need all the help you can get. To avoid any problems, put it in writing, take your time and make sure your roommate is the type you can communicate with should a problem arise.

Wherever you decide to live, be selective, be careful and stand strong at your door. Without a home, a place to call your own, you have little hope of building a new life.

Relocating

It takes courage to make the decision to disappear and relocate. It also takes know-how. Your local shelter should be able to inform you of the ways you can go about protecting yourself from being found by the man you want to get away from. In emergency situations, they can literally whisk you into an underground network that has connections all over the country. This, however, is *never* publicized or even disclosed even to most staff working in these organizations. You'll probably need to talk to the director or call one of the national shelter hotlines listed in this book in the resource section. Do not let anyone tell you it does not exist. Be insistent. You may have difficulty obtaining this information for it is well-guarded but there is not a shelter in this country that would not know what you are talking about. It's just a matter of getting to the right people. If you can, attend a support group that is part of a shelter's outreach program and talk to one of the counselors there. They can help you make a plan, advise you what to watch out for and connect you to services in your new location.

As to where you can relocate, consider moving to a small town or medium sized city if you are currently living in a large one. Make sure it is as far away as you can get. Living in huge cities makes it difficult to make new friends, feel safe and secure. Of course it is a matter of preference, but do understand that in today's world, large cities are the worst places to be. The crime rates, diseases, poor air quality and alienation (many people do not even know their own neighbor) can add to the stress you already have. You need friends, a place to grow a garden or keep a pet. You need to build a support network where people really know you and care about you and your children. If you are concerned about your financial survival in these smaller places, investigate the possibilities. A superb source of information in this regard is the book, *Country Bound!* by Marilyn and Tom Ross (Communication Creativity, 1992 P.O. Box 909 425 Cedar Street Buena Vista, CO 81211 Telephone (719) 395-8659). Their book consists of over four hundred pages of information, advice, resources and practical tips. There are more ways to create an income for yourself than you ever dreamed of. It certainly is worth investigating.

To protect your new found freedom after you move, consider these security measures:

- Use a private mail box service to receive your mail, not a post office box or your private residence.

- Don't put your home address on your checks or business cards.

- Don't use credit cards

- Get an unlisted telephone number

- List your utilities under the name of your property trust or someone else's name

- Call your friends and creditors and ask them to change your address to an address in another city, one in which you do not live. Arrange for someone there to forward mail to your private mail box. You can get a company to do it for you such as Mailboxes U.S.A. for example, if you do not have an individual.

- Get a new driver's license and put your private mail box address on it. Use the term, "Suite # instead of "P. O. Box".

- Watch your children. Abusers often track down their ex-partners through schools where the children are registered. Notify the office of the possibility so they *do not* give out any information.

- Always use your common sense when it comes to your safety. Even if you feel your abuser does not know where you are, stick to basic personal security measures such as not isolating yourself, locking your car, watching the whereabouts of your children at all times, not opening your door unless you know who it is and a whole array of other things you can do to protect yourself. Learn about it. Study it. Be aware. Stay safe and alive.

When asked what the best thing was that women could do to promote goals of the women's movement, Peggy Cleveland, a feminist theologian and writer, replied, "Help women get money."

Kim Klein
Fundraising For Social Change (Chardon Press, 1988)

Chapter 8

For the Love of Money

If every abused woman in America were to receive the sum of $100,000 cash, their numbers would decrease significantly. Economic dependence and fear of poverty play a large part in the reasons women do not leave abusive men, and there is no help more difficult to obtain than financial. There are many avenues of psychological assistance avaiable at low cost or no cost at all, but when it comes to just about everything else, money is required.

Legal aid, medical services, temporary shelter and food are available with patience and persistence, though none of these rank high in quality. Money for a home, proper equipment like a car, presentable clothes, dental care, day care, education, home furnishings, pet care and personal grooming costs is not readily available at all.

For many women, even well-meaning friends and family are loathe to give more than meets the minimum requirements. In a world where everyone she meets has a home, an income, and self-esteem, the abused woman trying to rebuild her life often stands alone. The only people she shares her predicament with are the women she meets in support groups, shelters and in counseling clinics.

Her doctor usually goes home to an elegant house and fine food. So does her lawyer. Her therapist, too, normally enjoys a life of basic security and ease. Personnel at various agencies and organizations she meets during the course of her daily ritual also have homes and wages. The author of every book about abuse she reads is well compensated and so are the talk show hosts such as Phil Donahue and Oprah Winfrey, who do so much to bring the plight of women like herself to the public's attention. And, most unfair of all, her abuser goes on to live his life, rarely suffering any financial loss at all.

Most people would not think of lending her a few thousand dollars or more to help her get on her feet, or giving her a car. There are those she knows, some of them relatives, who can. She argues with herself that she should not expect people to give her money or things. After all, they are not responsible for her. They may think she is lazy and only wants things for nothing. Maybe she's not worth it. She struggles on through a maze of court and public assistance papers, lengthy rules and regulations at shelters, donated clothes and expired food, knowing this experience has scarred her for life and wondering if perhaps it was better not to have left him at all.

We live in a society that is largely selfish and unfeeling for those who have no money. "Nobody loves you if you are down and out," is more true in America than anywhere else in the world. Very few people, especially those in the mental health professions, care to discuss with an abused woman what to do about the lack of money in her life. They fear having to give. Robin Norwood, a rare woman and the author of *Women Who Love Too Much* stated, "One reason that I have chosen to leave my practice as a therapist is that I have come to the point in my life where I can no longer charge a fee for sharing with others the tools that saved my life and yet were given to me free...they are a gift that comes from a Power greater than ourselves—to us and through us, but never from us. One of the greatest privileges of having been given these tools is sharing them with others."

Almost everyone leaves the burden of finances to helping organizations who simply are not equipped to give significant amounts to each individual. We do not live in a society where neighbor helps neighbor, families stick it out together, churches take care of their own, friends are friends for life or take the attitude, "she's not heavy, she's my sister." At least not when it comes to money. And today, when so many more women are leaving abusive men even though it spells poverty, society appears to be giving even less on a one-to-one basis, evident by the ever increasing numbers of homeless women.

Real hope for women leaving or attempting to leave torturous relationships can only come from those close to them, not from a dependence on charity or government aid. These things can mean a beginning, but they cannot financially carry them to a semblance of independence and pride.

If one person lifted a woman up, and then another did the same, and then another... there would be no more need for agencies at all. Or perhaps if everyone gave a little bit to one woman until she was independent, and she in turn gave to someone like her, she could carry on and help another, and so on.

The following are just a few ways we can help women break free from the violence and build new lives:

- A cab driver can offer free transportation to one woman on the run instead of leaving her on the street just because she cannot pay her fare.

- A dentist can replace one woman's teeth at no charge.

- A physician can give up his fee for one battered woman in an emergency situation.

- Instead of selling an unwanted car, it can be donated to a woman at a shelter.

- An apartment owner can rent a unit at no charge until income is established.

- Cash could be collected at places of work and given to a co-worker trying to leave an abusive husband.

- A therapist could counsel one woman in trouble without asking for payment.

- A day care center can take care of one woman's children at no charge.

There are so many ways to help abused women. Most of us know at least one woman who is victimized and struggling to free herself. Too often we turn away. Giving even a little bit, even to just one, can make all the difference.

Public Assistance

If you have to apply, try to remember Whoopi Goldberg did it and so did Sally Jesse Raphael. Just grit your teeth, don't waste your emotions feeling ashamed or like the world's biggest loser, but do what you have to do. There have been so many successful people in this country who have suffered on welfare at one time or another, that feeling bad about it is a waste. If you really need it, get it.

Be prepared for long waits, mounds of paper work and your usual run of rude, incompetent social workers, along with the kind, compassionate ones. A good worker can speed things up for you and help you understand what you are eligible for. If you should end up with someone who resents his or her job or feels overworked and underpaid, your life for a while just may be hell. However, even the worst of them eventually pull through for the simple fact you are entitled to receive aid if you have no food or home and no income.

After you make an appointment to see a worker, take with you every known document you think might be important—birth certificates, social security cards, previous income statements, tax returns, marriage or divorce papers, medical information if you are ill, rent receipts, utility bills, telephone bills, proof of address if you have one, court documents, custody papers and bank statements. There may be others, however you will be asked to send them in if you do not have them with you. The paper work is enormous and the waiting time to finally get benefits may be long, but there are allowances if you need emergency aid.

One word of caution: if you have children, try not to bring them. Waiting hours, sometimes half a day in large city offices, can be much too hard on a child. If you must bring your children, take toys and something for them to eat or drink.

Getting public assistance can help you get yourself back on your feet. At times you may receive a partial subsidy should you get a part-time job or are training for employment. Ask what is available and use it. At this point in your life it is going to take all you can to pull yourself together. Remeber this, however. Staying on welfare for too long can cost you your independence and your pride. You are never free, never in control. The system controls you and dictates how you live. Your food stamps may or not be there every month. You are at the mercy of the hands that control the computer. Being on welfare always leaves you with the question, "will I get it this month? Am I cut off?" It's not very different from being batttered. Is he going to hit me today?" He may or may not. Don't let yourself be at the mercy of his fists or their financial aid.

"If ever I loved...it was a child. If ever I hated...it was an adult. Yet the two are one and the same."

Chapter 9

Children:
The Innocents We Love

Children Caught In The Middle

It is estimated that about 50% of men who abuse women also abuse their children. Threatening to take the children away, abusing them physically, sexually and emotionally, are all attempts to control and intimidate.

The abuser's final extreme act of domination is to kill his partner or children or both. What is alarming and inconceivable is the fact that each year the numbers of men who are murdering not only their mates, but their children as well, are increasing. Startlingly enough, these men often commit suicide immediately after, or seem completely unconcerned that they will spend the rest of their lives in prison if convicted.

Here are some brutal facts:

- 2.9 million cases of child abuse were reported in the United States in 1992. Forty-five percent involved neglect, seventeen percent involved sexual abuse, twenty seven percent involved physical abuse, seven percent emotional abuse and eight percent were classified as "other" which includes abandonment (National Committee for the Prevention of Child Abuse, 1993).

- 12,261 children died of physical abuse and neglect in 1992 (National Committee for the Prevention of Child Abuse).

Please Don't Let Him Hurt Me Anymore

- Of the homeless women and children in the United States, up to half of them are fleeing from domestic violence (Elizabeth Schneider, *Legal Reform Efforts for Battered Women,* 1990)

- For every case of abuse reported, it is estimated that 200 are never exposed (From the book, *Sociology of Marriage and Family).*

- Nationwide, the government reported 4 children a day are killed by their parents or guardians, a 54% jump in the last 6 years *(Los Angeles Times, 1993).*

- 3.3 million children in the United States, between the ages of 3 and 17 years are at risk of exposure to parental violence each year (Peter Jaffe, David Wolf & Susan Day Wilson, *Children of Battered Women,* 1990).

- Generally, 70% of the men who abuse their female partners also abuse their children (Bowker, Arbitell & McFerron, "On The Relationship Perspectives Between Wife and Child Abuse," in *Feminist Perspectives on Wife Abuse,* Kersti Yllo & Michelle Bogard, eds., 1988).

- Reports by battered women show that in 87% of cases, children witness the abuse (Lenor Walker, *The Battered Women Syndrome,* 1984).

The atrocities committed against children are so grim that even those in the helping professions have difficulty coping with the reality of it. Children are burned, slapped, punched, drowned, smothered, shot, stabbed, beaten and hit with objects such as belts, sticks, paddles and brooms. They are also sexually abused in bizarre, painful ways, so shocking and sickening that it defies the senses.

Children are also very affected by witnessing the

constant abuse to which their mothers are subjected and need counseling after they are removed from the environment to prevent them from acting out the same things when they are adults.

Nothing seems to incite a public rage in this country more than the abuse of children. Yet it happens over and over in incredible numbers. The many laws and agencies working to prevent and correct this problem hardly seem to make a dent in solving it. On a personal level, it appears that most adults do not listen to their children, or somehow give them the message it is not safe to tell them the truth about incidents of abuse. Much more adult education is needed on how to raise children. For women who are abused, there is no answer but to get their children out.

We don't own our children the way we own such things as a house. Children are completely innocent and dependent upon us for their survival and protection. They need to be respected, guided and loved.

If you and your children are being abused, get help.

The following attempts to answer some vital questions about child sexual abuse.

Child Sexual Abuse

We all tend to assume that it is a stranger who abuses children sexually, however statistics show that it is most often parents, baby-sitters, family friends or relatives, or school employees who inflict this horror on our precious innocents. Since often no physical signs of sexual abuse are apparent, parents may be unsure their child has been through this experience. But remember, the most important factor in helping your child in any area of concern is your relationship with them. Do they talk to you? Do you listen to them? If they do not confide in you and trust you, even when they think they have done something wrong, it's time to evaluate precisely how well you are parenting. Very young children of course are unable to verbalize that they have been molested.

The following indicators can help you detect abuse:
- Physical discomfort in sitting or walking

- A sexually transmitted disease

- Poor appetite

- Insecurity

- Clinging behavior

- Changes in behavior that have no explanation

- Isolation

- Fear of particular places or people

- Bedwetting

- Excessive masturbation

- Acting out the abuse with toys, friends or through drawings

- Symptoms of stress.

Although the behaviors and signs listed above are commonly displayed by children who have experienced sexual abuse, some of them are fairly common indicators of other problems and parents should consider what other things might possibly explain these changes. Jumping to conclusions too quickly can sometimes do more damage than good. Sometimes you have to live with the fact that you just aren't sure. The most logical thing to do is prevent it in the first place. That means making your kids strong, self-confident and communicative. Discussions about preventing sexual abuse and facts about danger can be part of the normal things you teach your children. Stressing this too much can make children afraid of adults when they need not be. Even if you do not talk to them explicitly about sexual contact, provide the message that if anyone touches them or does anything that makes them uncomfortable, they should tell you or another trusted adult. Children should feel confident that they can say "NO" if they are asked to do something they don't feel right about, even if it is a relative, even if it is you. And if they do come to you with questions that alarm you, stay calm and answer them matter-of-factly.

If your child is often in the care of others, be sure to stay aware of other types of abuse. Examine your child's body routinely. A sensitive parent will notice any suspicious marks, bruises, burns or welts etc. If the child is not yours, look for inappropriate clothing for the season, hunger, a dirty hair and skin, limping, painful motions, and lack of supervision. These can be signs of a neglected or mistreated child and deserve attention.

If you suspect child abuse the following agencies may aid you in these specific areas:

- If you think a child is being abused by someone you know, such as a relative, neighbor, or friend, call the Police, Social Services or your city or county Department of Child Welfare.

- If a child has been attacked by a stranger, call the Police or Sheriff's Department.

- If you suspect a daycare, school, or recreational facility of any kind of child abuse, call the Police, Sheriff or your state or local Community Care Licensing authority.

- For information or complaints having to do with licensing, organization, staffing or programs of a licensed child care setting, call your state or local Community Care Licensing authority.

The Effects of Domestic Violence On Children

There was an incident where I found myself in the heart-wrenching position of having to pick up a woman who wanted out of her abusive relationship. I agreed to drive to her house and from there bring her to the intake office where she would be taken to a shelter for battered women. She had come to one of our support groups just once and we had exchanged telephone numbers. I was not surprised when she called me to get her. She said her husband was there with her two children, ages three and five. I was apprehensive about the possibility of violence but she reassured me her husband was calm because she had agreed not to take the children. He would let her go, but not them. Her plan was, she told me, to get herself established then get a court order to get them out. It was the only thing she could do. Afraid she would die during one his rages, she couldn't stay any longer. Tess was pale and thin, just a wisp of a woman that I could see was once buoyant, optimistic and full of life.

He sat and watched us cart out her few belongings. Half glaring, half in obvious emotional pain, he guarded their two children standing beside his chair. They did not move, only watched us with dark, frightened eyes. Just before I closed the door, I turned once more to look at the three of them. Those two sweet faces, so innocent, so pained and bewildered, I can never forget. What would happen to them with him? Tess assured me he never harmed them. He only beat her. Did they witness it? Yes. What would they do without their mother? How could we leave them? My feelings were so strong for these two little ones, I had the fleeting thought, "If only I could adopt them, right now, here... I'd never leave them."

Tess never made it. She returned three weeks later, leaving the shelter, disillusioned about what they could do for her. Without money, she felt there was no hope.

128

Her options at that time were legal aid and welfare. She couldn't stay away from her children. As for me, I never dared to look back. I moved shortly after and never contacted her again. I didn't have what she needed. Finances. I would have given her all that I had, but I didn't have it to give. I felt so helpless. I grieved. How I grieved.

I never needed a textbook to tell me the effect domestic violence has on children. I saw it myself; children with cigarette burns on their legs and arms; children so withdrawn a touch would make them recoil; children who didn't laugh or play anymore; children who were angry and struck out; young boys who were already displaying abusive characteristics towards women; infants who cried at the slightest noise, their little hands clenched, wailing into the night; drawings that spoke of terror, fires, black ominous clouds that surrounded their tiny selves on paper. The damage is obvious. It is ugly, senseless and at times, irreversible.

Children in abusive situations witness an array of behavior demonstrated by their parents that is both confusing and traumatic. They hear screams, threats, crashing noises. They see their father throwing their mother against walls, doors or onto the floor. They see him pounding her with his fists until she bleeds, kicking her, choking her or cutting her. Often the children themselves are victims of the same treatment.

Emotionally, children feel abandoned because their mother is fighting for her own survival and cannot defend them. She may try. They on the other hand, cannot help her either. The feel powerless, guilty and anxious. They are afraid they will lose their mother and their father. In a constant state of stress, these children are afraid to sleep in peace, ready to run at an instant's notice. Their home becomes a battleground, a place where it is not safe. Anything, could happen at any time. The never have the luxury of experiencing tranquillity, security or glee. Life becomes somber, dark and serious.

Children usually take the lessons they learn in these violent family situations with them into adulthood. Feelings of powerlessness can create a man who is obsessed with controlling others so he feels powerful, or a woman who continues to feel helpless and attracts people into her life who will abuse her. The ability to form close relationships is hindered, children growing up shy, not having the ability to trust others. Fear of abandonment, fear of being hurt in so many ways causes isolation and an unwillingness to share intimacies and real love. Low self-esteem shuts the door to any possibilities of genuine love in adults who have been children of parents who created a home life of fear and hate, victim and abuser. And how did they learn this treacherous dance? From their parents.

For adults who have witnessed domestic violence as children, the most damaging result is the inability to love. They do not feel love for themselves nor for others. They cannot be compassionate, feel empathy, care, or *feel* emotions of joy, generosity, genuine happiness for another's success and well-being. It is so blatantly absent and cannot be ignored that, even when these adults go through the motions of an apparently loving relationship, you know it is not real. It's like the song *Paper Roses*. It's just not real.

Looking into the face of an abusive man is a difficult thing for me to do. I am torn between the violent man and the innocent darling who was abused. I don't just see one. I see both the child and the adult. It is the same for a woman who has been victimized. She wasn't born to be abused. She possessed a joyful, healthy natural self-love as a new born. Until she learned otherwise.

When you help the children, you help the world.

The rain is famous for falling on the just and unjust alike, but if I had the management of such affairs I would rain softly and sweetly on the just, but if I caught a sample of the unjust outdoors I would drown him.

Mark Twain

Chapter 10

Attorneys, the Law and the Police

The Right Lawyer

You will need an effective lawyer to free yourself legally from your abuser. This point can't be emphasized strongly enough. The skillful lawyer is an essential necessity in any legal proceeding regarding your abusive state. Finding the right attorney to protect your legal rights, your sanity, and, in the extreme, but unfortunately all too frequent, cases, your life and/or the lives of your children is one of the most crucial decisions you will ever make. When the time finally comes for you to leave the abuser permanently, to break the chain of violence and intimidation once and for all, it is vital that you obtain proper legal representation to safeguard your steps out. We have all heard the tired platitude, "a good man is hard to find." Painfully, for the battered woman, a good lawyer may be the hardest to find.

But you must look for a lawyer and you cannot stop searching until you have found the right one for you. An attorney should be empathetic, supportive, vigorous, and reasonable in cost. Fairness and the law should be uppermost in your attorney's mind. He or she must inform you of all your legal rights and the problems and risks involved in obtaining restraining orders, in carrying through divorce proceedings, and in securing custody rights. A competent attorney will know all the proper legal steps and will know how and when to implement them.

Any lawyer who is only interested in how much you can pay or who pries too closely into your business or financial affairs should be avoided. A bad lawyer, one who doesn't truly appreciate or even correctly perceive your situation, a lawyer who takes advantage of your situation to shamelessly exploit what resources you do have is a blight to be avoided at all costs. That lawyer should also be reported to the proper legal governing board. Remember, a careless, greedy lawyer who might be swayed by your abuser's more pricey and high-profiled attorney may wind up costing you everything in court you are trying to achieve: custody of your children, alimony payments, and your share of a property settlement.

The point is this: be selective and cautious in choosing your attorney. Look carefully until you find the one who will work best for you. You are the one hiring the lawyer, the lawyer is not hiring you. In most cases, you are certainly paying the lawyer's salary. Don't take the first one who comes down the road offering quick and easy solutions. You already know that the solutions to abuse are not easy. Shop around. Compare. Use common sense, listen to what people tell you, ask questions you want answers to. If you hire an attorney and then find yourself unhappy or unsatisfied with that attorney, for whatever reason, do not hesitate to change. After all, you're not marrying a lawyer, only hiring one.

The United Sates is home to 70% of the world's practicing attorneys. The right lawyer is there for you once you know how and where to look. The first barrier you must cross is being able to speak up for yourself. Tell any prospective lawyer what you want, what you need, and what you expect. Remember, you are interviewing the lawyer to find out if he or she is right for you.

Attorneys, the Law and the Police

Who to approach first

Go to any lawyer you might already personally know. That lawyer can refer you to an attorney in the battering/abuse area.

Ask friends, family members, neighbors, co-workers, or employers for an attorney recommendation. Again, the lawyer who is recommended to you by someone you know may then refer you to the proper attorney.

Contact any professional person you know who might be able to recommend a lawyer. These people include bankers, doctors, ministers, social workers or teachers. Anyone in a professional capacity who may be able to refer you to an attorney is worth talking to.

Where to look on your own

The Yellow Pages of your local phone book contain listings for legal referral services under the headings "Attorney Referral Services," "Attorneys," or "Lawyers." Call an attorney, explain your situation, ask who you should contact. Make an appointment. You can speak to a lawyer for half an hour for a small fee.

The Yellow pages also contain advertisements for specific legal services. Lawyers advertise, and they make it very clear the type of clients they're trying to acquire. Check local newspaper ads for the same services.

Contact nonprofit public interest organizations such as a civil liberties agency or a housing discrimination agency. Both will have staff lawyers who may be able to help you. Use the white pages of the phone book to find these agencies.

Federal, State, or County agencies in social services and welfare can also steer you to the proper legal service.

Community newspapers, radio stations and television stations may offer legal "action hot lines." Use them.

If you belong to a "legal insurance" plan through employment or as an individual, your plan will offer lawyers to contact. In most cases, these plans feature special low attorney's rates

Free help in noncriminal cases can be obtained from Legal Aid Societies or Legal Services Foundations for women who cannot afford a lawyer. Check the white pages of your phone book for these services. Know that even if you obtain free legal service, you may still incur any court costs involved.

If for some reason you are accused of committing a crime and can't afford a lawyer, contact the local Public Defender's office in your county through your white pages. The court will also appoint you a private attorney at no charge in such cases.

Free or low-cost legal help may also be obtained through a Lawyer Referral Service or from law school "clinic" programs.

Just like doctors, some lawyers do specialize. If a lawyer has qualified as a "certified specialist" under your state bar specialization program, it means that he or she has experience and tested ability in one or more fields of law. Only these lawyers may advertise themselves as certified specialists. Look for their ads in the Yellow Pages or newspapers, or write your state board of legal specialization for a list.

Knowing which attorney is best

After you've "comparison shopped," make a list of several lawyers and then phone the ones on your list. Ask them for information that will help make your decision. The lawyer's secretary may be able to provide you the information you need. Some attorneys may want to meet with you briefly instead of discussing your problem on the phone. Even if a lawyer you speak with does not normally deal with cases like yours, you may still be able to get the help you need from that lawyer. That's why the interview you conduct with a lawyer is so important.

Questions to ask a lawyer initially

- How much experience do you have in cases like mine?

- How recently have you handled a similar case?

- How long do you think my case might take?

- Do you charge for a first consultation?

- What is your basic fee?

- How will I be charged?

Take notes on everything each lawyer says. Write it all down. Take the time to think their responses over, then make a formal appointment with the attorney who seems right for you.

Hiring the attorney

You won't know whether you want to hire a lawyer or not until after your first meeting. Don't make a decision on the spot unless you're absolutely certain. Before your first meeting, make notes so you can go over the important points of your case with the lawyer. Bring the names, addresses and telephone numbers of everyone connected with your case. Bring all papers involved in your case. Ask the attorney to describe cases like yours that he or she may have handled. Ask if the attorney will handle your case personally. If the attorney feels another member of the firm should handle any part of your case, ask to speak with the second attorney as well.

Keep in mind that no legal matter is a "sure thing." No lawyer can guarantee results. Avoid lawyers who do. A good lawyer will be able to explain all the strengths and weaknesses of your case to you. He or she will lay it all out for you. If you don't understand what the lawyer tells you, ask for an explanation in simpler language. Be clear on everything a lawyer tells you.

Questions to ask yourself

- Will I be comfortable working closely with this lawyer?

- Does the lawyer have the experience and skill to handle my case?

- Do I understand the lawyer's explanation of what my case involves?

- Does the fee seem reasonable?

If your answer is "no" to one or more of these questions, go to another lawyer. If all your answers are "yes," you may have found the right one.

The lawyer's fees

In order to arrive at a proper fee, a lawyer will consider the amount of time he or she thinks your case might require. The lawyer will figure in his or her own operating costs, including office rent, utility bills, staff salaries, office equipment and research materials. All professional people operate this way.

A lawyer may need to spend more time on your case than you might think. This will all be reflected in the fee that is charged. Unanticipated complications in your case will increase the fee. Some lawyers charge the "going rate," while others, who may be more well known or who are specialists, may charge more. You will have to weigh a lawyer's fee against his or her perceived skill and experience before you make a decision to hire a particular attorney. Sometimes a more expensive lawyer will lead to better and faster results in your case, sometimes not.

Not all attorneys charge the same way. Ask for a written fee agreement or letter that will spell out how much the lawyer will charge and what the charges will include. It may be impossible for a lawyer to know exactly how much time your case will take. Unexpected developments may effect the time allotted. Your agreement can include an "estimate" of the costs and time involved. This could prevent a major misunderstanding later.

Excluding a charge for your first meeting, the lawyer you hire will ask for a "fixed," "hourly," "retainer," "contingency," or "statutory" fee for your case.

Fixed fee

This is sometimes called a "standard" fee arrangement. It covers most routine legal matters. Legal clinics and some law firms and lawyers use this arrangement. When you agree to a fixed fee, be sure you know what it does and does not include and what other charges might be added later.

Hourly fee

Some lawyers prefer to charge by the hour. The hourly amount can vary from lawyer to lawyer. Ask the lawyer to estimate the amount of time your case will take. If you contact three lawyers and one charges more than the other two, you will have to decide for yourself if that lawyer's skills can expedite your case enough to warrant the higher charge.

Retainer fee

A retainer fee arrangement usually means that additional legal fees will also be billed to the client. A retainer fee is a "holding" fee. It guarantees a lawyer's availability to take a particular case. It sometimes means a lawyer will turn down other business to concentrate on the case at hand. It also means the client should expect to be billed separately for the legal work performed. A retainer usually covers a set period of time. In some instances, some of the legal work may be covered under the retainer. Many lawyers view a retainer as nothing more than a "down payment" on legal services a client needs.

Contingency fees

This arrangement means you will pay your attorney a fixed percentage of any money you receive if you win a court case or settle out of court. This type of fee usually occurs when you sue someone for money. If you lose, the lawyer receives no fee and you will have to pay court costs and other expenses. However, even if you win, you will still be responsible for court costs and expenses. Any out-of-pocket money paid by your lawyer will eventually be paid by you.

If you enter a contingency fee arrangement, know at the outset what your lawyer's fees will be. Make sure you clearly understand whether the lawyer's fee will be paid before or after court costs are deducted. If your lawyer's fee is paid *after* court costs are deducted, you will receive more money and the attorney less money than if the fees is payed *before* costs are deducted. Remember that court costs come out of your pocket, not the lawyer's. If the fee is paid after costs, the lawyer's percentage derives from monies left, not from the original settlement amount.

If you're in a contingency situation with your attorney, you may be involved in a "cross complaint." In other words, the person you are suing is suing you. This means more work for your attorney and also a higher fee.

Statutory fee

The cost of certain type of legal work is preset by "statute" or law. In some cases, the court will set or approve the fee you pay your lawyer.

Summary

In most cases involving abuse, you most likely will be faced with a choice of a fixed, hourly, or retainer fee situation when hiring your attorney. Whatever fee arrangement you strike with your lawyer, make sure that all legal services and charges are spelled out in writing beforehand. You want a signed and dated written agreement or formal letter of engagement. Do not enter into any legal situation with an attorney without full disclosure of what is to take place and how much it is to cost.

Working With Your Lawyer

The most important aspect of your relationship with your attorney is mutual honesty. Be candid. Tell your lawyer everything you know. Expect your lawyer to tell you everything. Your lawyer cannot do the job for you if you hold anything back. This means disclosing information you may feel is not important or that you may feel is even harmful to your case. The lawyer has to know. Report any and all new developments to your attorney immediately. If the lawyer needs your assistance in gathering all papers together and in collecting any other evidence or in lining up any witness you may need to testify, be willing to do whatever is necessary. It's your case. Be an active participant.

Keep in mind that timetables may be difficult for your lawyer to establish. He or she may set an approximate timetable for the unfolding of events in your case, but circumstances such as crowded court schedules can interfere. Ask your attorney for regular, periodic updates. Also ask for copies of any letters or documents prepared for your case. If you have questions as your case proceeds, call your lawyer. At the same time, keep in mind that depending on the fee arrangement, your lawyer may charge you for any time spent in talking with you.

Problems With Your Lawyer

You have a number of options if you are unhappy or unsatisfied with the attorney you have hired.

The first thing to do is to speak up. If you don't like

the way your case is being handled, tell the lawyer what you want done differently. If you want more verbal contact with the lawyer, say so. If you can't work out a solution for whatever reason, change attorneys. However, expect to pay for the legal work your current lawyer has performed for you.

If you have a disagreement with your attorney over the fee and can't settle the problem yourselves, take your dispute to an impartial arbitration panel. Even a signed fee agreement can be arbitrated. Don't hesitate to act in the case of a dispute.

If you believe your attorney has deliberately mishandled your case or has been dishonest in conduct with you in any other way, the State Bar of the state in which you live will investigate a complaint. Any lawyer found guilty of professional misconduct can be punished. Client security funds exist in many states. If you have lost money because of your lawyer's misconduct, you can recover a portion of it. In extreme cases, you may also sue your own attorney for "malpractice." Even if your lawyer makes an honest mistake, you may still take your complaint to court.

This situation, thankfully, will not occur in most cases. Attorneys and clients generally have good relationships. Any attorney who protects your legal rights and perhaps directly, your life and the lives of your children, is worth his or her weight in gold. The point to keep in mind is that you need decent legal representation when you leave your abuser. No amount of effort on your part in seeking an able attorney is too small. It could mean all the difference in changing your life for good.

Restraining Order

You do not need a lawyer's help in obtaining a restraining order from court that will tell your abuser to stay away from you.

Restraining orders come in two types: temporary and permanent. You must go to court at least twice to obtain both. The temporary order lasts about 20 days, and the permanent order lasts for up to three years. The first time in court, the temporary order is issued. Then, following the court hearing, the permanent order is issued.

The papers you receive and that your abuser receives will advise you both to seek an attorney in any matter connected with the restraining order application.

Though you do not need an attorney to obtain the temporary order, it will be much easier to obtain the permanent order if you have an attorney. Free help from a lawyer is available to everyone. You do not have to show that you are poor. To obtain this free service go to your district Superior Court. Identify yourself to the bailiff as needing free legal aid. Your name will most likely be put on a waiting list, and then you will be called. Days and times of lawyer availability will be given to you. Call to confirm that a volunteer will be available the next day. Arrive early, because help is usually on a first come, first served basis.

Getting the abuser to pay

If you think your abuser will hire an attorney to fight the restraining orders, you should have your own attorney to protect your interests. If you don't have time to stand in line for free legal aid because of work or other considerations, then hire an attorney to draw up the necessary papers. Do not enter any legal situation in which your abuser has an attorney and you do not.

Make sure your lawyer stipulates in your court papers that the abuser will pay your attorney's fees and court costs. If you prevail at your hearing, the judge in most states will be required to order the abuser to pay your fees and costs.

The way in which you can greatly aid your attorney is by writing out in detail the incidents of abuse.

Example:

"Last Tuesday, on April   , 199 , at approximately 8:30 a.m., the Defendant struck me in the face with his fists. We were in the kitchen. Our seven year old daughter and our five year old son were watching."

If you fully detail the incidents of abuse in writing, it will save your lawyer a considerable amount of time and it will save you money. You should view this as another instance of active participation in your own case.

In some cases, your attorney can get the temporary restraining order for you without your having to go to court. It may be that you only have to be present in court at the hearing to determine the permanent three year order.

When in the restraining order phase, in almost all cases, it benefits you to have a lawyer. An attorney will protect your legal rights and ensure that the abuser pays your fees and costs. This is what you want: the abuser to start paying for his abuse.

Relief under a temporary restraining order

The temporary restraining order, which lasts from 20 to 25 days, provides relief for you, the filing party, from your abuser.

An abuser may be prohibited from continuing further forms of abuse against you in the following ways:

- Contacting

- Molesting

- Attacking

- Striking

- Threatening

- Sexually assaulting

- Battering

- Disturbing the peace

The temporary order will cover anyone named in the papers, including you and any other family or household members you name. This means the abuser must stay away from your children or anyone else you care to protect.

This order may also include *residence exclusion*. The abuser may be excluded from the family dwelling or your dwelling, regardless of which party holds legal title to the property. If you show that the abuser has assaulted or threatened to assault you or any other person under your care, custody, or control of your minor children, the court may order the residence exclusion into effect as well.

Any violation of the temporary restraining order by the abuser against you may result in his arrest and/or in criminal charges being filed against him.

Relief under the permanent order

The same conditions will apply after the hearing in relation to the permanent order as applied under the temporary order.

In addition, other forms of restraint may be imposed on the abuser:

- *Property restraint:* the abuser may be prohibited from selling transferring or in any way encumbering any property except in the usual course of business.

- *Custody:* the abuser may be denied temporary custody of your minor children or even the right to visit the minor children of your marriage. The court will determine custody placement and any conditions regarding visitation rights. Supervised visitation could be a condition. If you are not or were not married to the abuser, the court will determine custody.

- *Child support:* if the court presumes the abuser is the father of a child from your marital relationship, child support may be awarded by the court.

- *Restitution:* the victim of abuse is only entitled to restitution under the Domestic Violence Prevention Act if:

  - you can prove as a *direct result* of the abuse or injuries sustained that you lost earnings; OR

  - you can prove as a *direct result* of the abuse or injuries sustained that you paid for medical care; OR

  - you can prove as a *direct result* of the abuse or injuries sustained that you paid for temporary housing.

The abuser may also be ordered by the court to make restitution to any agency that provided you or your family with services that were required as a *direct result* of abuse or the abuser's injurious actions.

The term *direct result* means what it implies. Judges strictly adhere to rigid parameters when applying the ruling. Physical manifestations of abuse with proper support, i.e., a doctor's order that you stay home from work for three days because of the injuries you sustained from your abuser, would most likely be regarded by a judge as a case of loss of earnings stemming from a *direct result* of abuse. Restitution would then, most likely, be awarded. But if you claim that emotional distress due to your abuser's threats kept you home from work for three days, a judge would be much less likely to find the loss of earnings as having stemmed from a direct result of abuse.

Rightly or wrongly, threats and intimidation do not hold the weight with judges that actual physical abuse does in terms of restitution.

Don't make a frivolous filing. If you seek restitution you are not entitled to, the chance of getting a lawyer's fees and court costs paid for by your abuser are greatly reduced. However, restitution and other damages not directly resulting from abuse or the injuries suffered from abuse may still be sought in a separate action. Ask you attorney to advise you in this area.

The court, finally, may also order your abuser to obtain counseling. This will only be placed under two conditions: if the abuser agrees to counseling OR if you show on your papers that:

- you intend to continue living in the same household

- you have continued to reside in the same household after previous instances of domestic violence.

In conclusion, when you proceed to the legal arena to fight your abuser, the most powerful weapon you can take into battle will be your attorney. You must have a skillful lawyer to guide you through the sometimes harrowing maze of courtroom proceedings. If your abuser has legal counsel, it is paramount that you have your own. Remember, you're fighting for your freedom, your sanity, your life. In many cases, you're fighting for the lives of your children. The only way to safeguard what you hold most dear in a court of law is through an attorney.

Police Protection

Having to call the police in the case of uncontrollable violence is traumatic and frightening. Many women do not want to call for various reasons but, when they do, it is because they are too frightened not to and it is their last resort. What the police can and cannot do for you in terms of protection varies from state to state.

Here are some basic points you should know:

- Once you place a call to 911 for help in a domestic dispute, you cannot call back and cancel it. It will do no good to tell them the fight is over or he is gone. The police will come to your home anyway. (This may not be true in all cities, but it is in Los Angeles.)

- Some police officers are sexist; others are genuinely concerned and helpful. Then there are those who are very, very mean.

- If your abuser has injuries or bruises, etc., it is possible you will be arrested for assault instead of him. One officer stated it this way, "Whoever gets to the telephone first and reports trouble is the one who is the victim."

- The police will not come to your home if you suspect danger. They will come only during or after a violent episode.

- It may take up to an hour for them to come after you call. It depends upon their availability.

- In 1991, 61,089 domestic violence calls were received by the Los Angeles Police Department (Department of Justice, Bureau of Criminal Statistics, Sacramento, California). 244,356 incidents of abuse went unreported (Councils on Family Violence). Eighty percent of incidents involving physical violence are not reported due to shame, fear or a need to protect the abuser.

- In some states, undocumented women, lesbians and women involved in crime may not be eligible to receive protection from the police at all because of existing laws.

- Just because you do not leave your abuser does not mean you are not entitled to protection.

- Most police officers can advise a woman of where to turn for basic assistance such as shelters and restraining orders. They can also drive you to a place of safety or to the hospital.

- There is no guarantee your partner will automatically be arrested if you call the police. It depends upon the law in your state and the interpretation of the situation by the officers.

It has been said that police officers do not like to go on domestic violence calls due to the dangers involved. Too often they are forced to shoot an individual, severely injuring or killing them, risking their own lives in the process. The horror of these situations must be devastating and most of us would find it hard to identify with how these officers must feel.

They are often faced with having to console frightened, bewildered children after a domestic dispute call, and many officers report being emotionally distraught themselves as a result of domestic violence calls.

Take the case of Arturo Buitron, 32, of Elverta, California, who was finally shot to death in his car by sheriff's deputies after leading them on a chase while hanging his one-year-old daughter from his car, threatening to kill her. After he crashed into a tree, it was reported deputies opened fire when it appeared he was stabbing the child. After an incident such as this, how do these men go on?

Can any one of us imagine what it must be like for these officers to arrive on the scene where Iliana Perez, 19, also of California lay on the ground, blood splattered all over her white wedding dress, just shortly after she was shot to death by her jealous former boyfriend? Not only was she dead just hours after her marriage to her new man, but her attacker, Salvador Mejia also lay dead beside her, having shot himself in the head. It is a sight few of us could stomach, yet one which police officers must steel themselves against week after week.

Although the police have been criticized many times for being too slow, too cold and unfair, they have at the same time not been given the credit they deserve. No, we often dislike and fear the police because of the few who hideously abuse their positions, but we shouldn't overlook those who have saved precious lives by tragically being forced to take another. And that's not an enviable position.

If you need them, don't hesitate to call the police for help. Chances are you'll get the good ones.

Chapter 11

Staying Safe, Secure and Alive

Personal Protection

Living with a man who severely abuses you, hounds you, threatens your sanity and your life and then won't let you go when you desperately want to leave, produces a feeling within you that is difficult to explain. It can be described with such words as terrifying, horrifying, anxiety provoking, nauseating, bittersweet or brutal, for example, but no words can truly ever be put on paper that could capture it. It consumes all of your being. It's like being sealed in a large glass tumbler with a sour, dark, sticky syrup constantly being forced down your throat which you cannot stop and which makes you gag. The flow of it fills you and fills you until you become it. You no longer feel the glass. Nothing exists but that flow of vile liquid in a prison that you cannot even see.

Women do get out. They shatter the glass and crawl out, but the memory of the feeling stays with them long after the relationship is over. Even then, so many of them live with the threat of being physically maimed or murdered for years and years after. Fear envelopes them like a heavy, gray cloud, their lives now consumed by obsessive thoughts of raw survival. It is very easy for those not involved to give the advice, "leave him," because they do not understand the consequences of doing so. Leaving him is one thing, staying alive is quite another.

Please Don't Let Him Hurt Me Anymore

Consider the following tragedies all of which occurred in California: October 12, 1993, North Hollywood- Following an evening family gathering, nine year old German Garcia was shot to death by his father, Miguel Garcia Manzo after Miguel Manzo flew into a rage when his former wife, Maria Chavez de Garcia 30, refused to reconcile with him. Wounded in the face and back by gunshots, she survived the brutal attack along with her other son, eleven year old Miguel Carcia Jr., but just barely. Miguel Manzo was described by stunned co-workers as "an excellent employee, a good person, dedicated to his sons." Although he had no criminal record, he savagely abused his wife to the point that she had to be admitted to the hospital. Other incidents of violence were not reported to police. Maria did all the right things. She left her abuser, was financially independent and raising two sons who according to school personnel were award winning students. Did she ever expect her ex-husband would kill one of their children and try to kill her and their other son? Obviously not or she wouldn't have allowed him to come into her home to visit them.

June 8, 1988, Dana Point-While sleeping in her bedroom Julie Alban was shot in the back by her boyfriend Bradley Ackerman. One day earlier she had rejected his proposal of marriage. Bradley, a former national junior tennis champion, shot himself in the chest right after wounding Julie but survived and later recovered. Julie however, became a paraplegic, the bullet still lodged in her spine today. Though suffering her great pain and experiencing intense depression, she overcame the odds. She graduated from the Western State University College of Law in Fullerton California and established a fund for law students in wheel chairs. Julie managed to stay alive after rejecting her abuser.

October 28, 1992, Long Beach-Extremely despondent after Victoria Lynn Myrick, 28, broke up with him, Robert Steven St. John 26, kidnapped her and killed her and himself in a motel room in Chico. A former Long Beach City College campus police officer, St. John had a prior conviction of keeping another woman a prisoner, and spoke of being extremely depressed after losing his girlfriend Victoria. She was "in extreme fear of her life" and had filed a restraining order.

The stories of women being stalked, harassed and murdered by men they loved fill our newspapers every day all over the country. It tells us something is profoundly wrong. Women do not know how to protect themselves, how to judge a man's potential for murder or what steps to take to have him stopped. There also appears to be a factor of incredulity as stated by one of Sally Jesse Rapheal's guests on one her programs in 1993. "Am I going to die?" she asked herself after being shot in the back three times by her former boyfriend and lying on the ground near the steps of her local police station. "I mean you deny getting shot because it's not normal and it's hard to believe."

If You're Being Stalked...
Incorporating some of the following guidelines will be very helpful in protecting yourself if you are being harassed, threatened and pursued by a dangerous man.

- File a Restraining Order and find about the stalking laws in your state. Use them.

- Have as little contact with your pursuer as possible. Do not go out in public by yourself. Notify everyone around you that you are in danger so they can warn you if he comes around. If he calls you, hang up. Don't be fooled into a meeting with him to work things out or believe promises of better behavior.

- Secure your residence with devices such as alarms, a dog, private patrol and brick walls.

- Document every single thing that he does when he tries to get at you. Use videotapes, tape recorders, private investigators and witnesses. These things will help you get a conviction in court.

- Be strong and do not show fear. Absolutely refuse to have any kind of relationship with him.

- Don't feel sorry for him.

- Find out about the laws regarding guns. If you are sure you can follow the law, know how and when to use this weapon and you feel confident in your ability to control it, get one. Use it only if it is the absolute last resort. Get proper training and if it ever becomes necessary to use it, aim to maim, not to kill. The law is harsh when it comes to murder and, self defense may be difficult to prove. You can destroy your whole life if you kill someone, not to mention the trauma of living with that fact for the rest of your life.

- Explore other self defense tactics such as mace, self-defense training and bodyguards.

- Join a support group.

- Invest in a car-phone.

- If all else fails, relocate and disappear. Call your local shelter to find out about networks to help you do it. Most of them have an underground contact system and they will help you.

Don't let anyone tell you there is no guarantee that you can protect yourself from someone who is threatening to harm or kill you. It depends on the depth of your will to live and that you stay conscious of the dangers. Don't brush it off or take chances. Let your intuition and dreams help you. If you have constant nightmares, pay attention. Listen to your feelings, even if they appear to be illogical. If you sense something is wrong, but can't explain it, follow your intuition.

It is you who ultimately will save your life. No one will be as vigilant, responsible and as assertive as you. That is true for all of us.

Bodyguards

Sweden is the only country in the world to provide funding for bodyguards for battered women. In the United States, the first agency specifically offering protection to abused women was started in Milwaukee, Wisconsin, by Gregory Kottke. Working closely with the local Task Force on Battered Women, the agency charges $30.00 an hour or, depending on the client's income, nothing at all.

In the Los Angeles area, AAA Protection Service Agency specializes in domestic violence and court appearances for women, as well as escorting them in situations which they feel are dangerous, such as returning to a hostile home to collect their belongings.

Because of the escalating violence against women, some security companies are waking up and finally accommodating women in the area of personal protection from their abusers. They are doing what the police and the court systems are not, and that is protecting them from being assaulted or murdered. *Preventing* abuse is the issue, not taking action against the abuser after the hideous damage is done, though that avenue is better than none.

The concept that we, as women, have to flee for our very lives from the men we marry and love, the men who are the fathers of our children, is so alien to a healthy, logical mind, that to take the step of hiring another man to protect us from them seems almost unbelievable. It insults our senses. Insanely, it does exist and this outrage must be stopped and women must learn to protect themselves. Hiring a trained bodyguard is one of the most effective ways to do this.

Guard dogs

According to Mel Mandell in his book, *Being Safe,* dogs have sharp hearing and sense of smell and that often makes them better detectors of intruders than electronic devices. Apart from attacking the person who is there to harm you, a dog also can frighten would-be intruders with its loud barking. In some cases this is effective enough to scare them off.

Dogs take time, money, discipline and patience. The cost involved in having a dog trained can be high, as well as the cost for feeding, veterinary care, etc. German Shepherds, female Dobermans, Bull Terriers and Rottweilers are good breeds to consider as guarg dogs. All dog owners should carry liability insurance and dogs should never attack except on command.

Be careful from whom you buy your dog and who trains it. Watch out for what may appear to be a bargain as not everyone is qualified to sell guard dogs. The most important thing, of course, is to get an animal that you are fond of and one that is intelligent.

Pepper spray

Almost all states have legalized the use of pepper spray, a sticky substance containing pepper which can burn an attacker's eyes, and render him or her helpless for over half an hour. At least helpless enough to stop the assault on the victim. Pepper spray creates a burning sensation and affects a person's ability to breathe. It does not however, cause serious or long term injury. Symptoms usually subside within ten to fifteen minutes and are entirely gone within an hour.

The spray is a welcome alternative for women who are uncomfortable with guns yet need protection, either from their abusers or possible assaults in parking lots or other unsafe areas. In California it is required that users first be certified either by watching a 30 minute videotape at local police stations or educational institutions or pass a written exam. Also, only certain brands of the spray are legal. Check your state laws to see which ones are available to you. The cost of a canister is approximately $15.00 to $20.00.

Private investigators

If you are being stalked by your former mate, or harassed and threatened, one of the best things you can do for yourself is to call a private investigator and have him followed so you know where he is all the time. It's called surveillance. Instead of living in fear that he may find you, turn it around and find him.

The agencies listed in the Resources section of this book are just a few that offer this wonderful service. Some of them provide bodyguards as well.

Don't be a victim. Don't sit there waiting and wondering. Don't live alone. Don't let things go on until you are so frightened you cannot function. Do not go out alone. Take some control of your situation and do what you can to *prevent* your abuser from harming you.

Basic home security

Even if your former mate does not know where you live, take precautions in case he does find you. Most women who are murdered by their partners, are killed after they leave. "It's a frightening fact," says Alana Bowman, assistant Los Angeles city attorney, "The woman must leave the violent situation without question. So all of us who work with domestic violence issues urge women to get out and make themselves safe, but it takes a lot of thought." (L.A. Life, Sunday July 3, 1994)

Here are some basic security tips for your home:

- Lighting fixtures outside your home should be made of plastic so they cannot be broken, leaving you without light outside. Exterior lights should be connected to a timer and located over accessible windows and doors.

- Prickly or thorny shrubbery are good deterrents against intruders. Place them near ground-floor windows.

- Know your neighbors. Alert them to any possible danger. Ask them to keep watch for you when you are away. Make sure they have your telephone number and you have theirs.

- Make sure every door has a lock on it. Doors should be thick, (at least 1 3/4 inches) and have a peephole. Glass portions of doors should be replaced with plastic that does not break or with security glass. One of the most terrifying things women experience is the sound of shattered glass from an attacker who is kicking the door down.

- Consider non-removable bars on your windows. (Make sure you can open them from the inside.)

- Window fans or air-conditioners should be bolted down.

- Garage doors should be locked. In all cases, use strong locks.

- Get an alarm system.

- Have a cellular telephone. This way your wires can never be cut You'll always be able to call out for help if there is trouble.

- In case the intruder cuts off your electricity, (it's been known to happen) you can help yourself with a battery lantern. This will light up a whole room by itself. Or install emergency power failure lights in your hallways and bedrooms.

If You Have To Run...

If you feel things are so dangerous that you have to flee your home and you don't have time to make a plan or prepare, grab all of your important papers, money, valuables, keys, telephone numbers of shelters, hotlines etc., your children and your pets and go. If you don't have a car, call a taxi, friend and or neighbor. Go to a hotel or motel and try to keep calm. *DO NOT LET ANY-ONE KNOW WHERE YOU ARE,* not even your best friend or relative. They may be accosted and forced to declare your whereabouts. Call everyone and warn them. Most abusers look for their missing wives at the homes of those she knows. *DO CALL HOTLINES OR AGENCIES EXPERI-ENCED WITH DOMESTIC VIOLENCE.* They can help you plan your next step. If you have no money, tell the motel you will pay in the morning, it is an emergency, or get one of the operators on the hotline to vouch for the bill for you. Some of them can pay it for you. If you are on the street, get to a phone booth and call a 24-hour hotline or your nearest shelter. Tell them you need emergency shelter. If all fails, call the police and tell them to get you to an emergency, temporary shelter. Tell them your life is in danger. Someone *will* help you.

There is nothing more beautiful to see than genuine love between a man and a woman.

From this springs the foundation of our society.

We must do all we can to encourage and preserve this love.

Chapter 12

Recovery: Is There Life, Love and Marriage After?

The road to freedom and independence is rocky. It is filled with potholes, bumps and ups and downs. You need to develop a whole new set of skills and attitudes. Employment, friends, housing, self-esteem and new men in your life become issues that previously may not have been a concern. It can be arduous and painful. It takes time, courage and a whole lot of support from wherever you can get it.

Women do not just simply sail away from abusive relationships. Some of them crawl, others run and there are those who physically raise themselves up and fight until their abuser never comes back. However they do it, those who manage to make it are happier, stronger and more successful than they were before. And many times, they marry again...to loving and supportive men.

The scars remain, the struggle to achieve happiness is often long, and memories and fears can take years of therapy to resolve. Setbacks and depression are common during recovery, but the madness of violence is gone for good. With that absence comes relief and the spirit blossoms.

Yes, there is life, love and marriage after. If you want to know for yourself, join a support group and ask the women there who have survived. Talk to them. Observe them. They are our living heroines, our hope and our strength.

A New Man

When the rage settles, understanding and wisdom penetrate and you are ready for a new man, make sure generosity is one of his main characteristics. Living with a man who is controlling and stingy is pure hell. Women involved with men who dictate a "closed wallet" policy live lives of pure lack, not only financially, but emotionally as well. It is a truth—men do not bond with sex, but with money.

A word about generosity

Understandably, the happiest women are those in relationships with generous men. For this kind of man, nothing is too good nor too much for you. He'd clean out his bank account to buy you the world, if he could. He'd give you everything he had—his heart, his home—just to be with you. Why? Because he loves you.

Do such men as these really exist?

Well...

Some of them come pretty darn close...

Few women would argue the fundamentals of a generous man. They're the kind you never have to ask— they offer. They do not use their money to control a woman nor do they expect payment for anything they may give. Generous men demonstrate concern for a woman's welfare and she never has to worry should she be in need. They are kind, thoughtful and tender-hearted, as generous with their emotions as their money. They don't need to be rich—they just share what they have.

There are many reasons women become involved with men who do not give, just as there are complex reasons not all women are honorable in their intentions with generous men. But a woman who loves and values herself will not settle for anything less than a genuine relationship with a noble man.

If your new man displays any of the following...
- Constantly "forgets" his wallet

- Neglects your birthday or anniversary

- Feigns poverty

- Haggles over prices in public

- Expects sex after giving a gift

- Never offers

- Mutters, "I'm broke" too often

- Tells you he forgot to go to the bank right in the middle of dinner in a restaurant

- Uses his money to control or manipulate

- Doesn't like to share his things

- Immediately asks "How much does it cost?" when you need something

- Never gives money to the needy

- Buys you expensive gifts then hands you the credit card bill at the end of the month

He is inconsiderate, thoughtless and demanding.

Avoiding the next abuser

Recognizing the following as warning signs of a potential abuser will not be hard for you now.

If any of these occur, do more than run. Get rid of him.
- He hits you

- He gets angry easily over small things

- He tries to isolate you

- He resents your success

Please Don't Let Him Hurt Me Anymore

- He does not communicate his feelings well
- He changes personality quickly
- He comes from a violent family
- He always blames you
- He has no empathy
- He gets violent when he drinks
- He has a history of violence with other women
- He tries to control you

The components of a non-violent relationship are trust, respect, honesty, fairness, non-intimidating behavior, shared responsibilities, positive parenting and economic partnership. What all this really says is to have relationship free of any kind of violence, there is love. And love is not hard to recognize. It *feels* good.

There are other important traits to look for when you decide on being with a new man. Compassion, kindness, intelligence, strength and honesty are just a few, but the most important one of all is that he possess the wisdom to allow you to be who you are and not be judgmental of you or try to change you. He may not always agree with you or like what you do, but there is a fundamental acceptance, respect and love for you which supports your struggle to grow, learn and find happiness.

This quality is very easy to recognize and it is not common. You will find a certain ease just being around a man like this, a peace you won't feel with most people. Someone wonderful once said, "What greater happiness could you ask for from anyone other than that they be content however they see happiness to be. Leave them alone. Love them. Let them have the opportunity to discern their own happiness. You simply enjoy your life and be: that is the greatest thing you can give them."

If you find a new man and you begin to have a desire to change him, and the things he does and says are gnawing at you and making you feel uncomfortable, he's the wrong man. Being with a man who brings up feelings of low self-esteem or anger or anxiety, even though you are attracted to him in many ways, is not a good prospect for a satisfying relationship. These are remnants of old patterns that have not been completely resolved and need more attention. Real self-love has not yet been attained, and it is wise to explore this further with a therapist.

Many women who have experienced abuse within their relationships never marry the same type of man again. There are other women, not the majority, who keep repeating the pattern and wind up with an abuser over and over again. The fear and pain they experienced compels them to seek men who do not inflict this upon them again. In order to achieve this, most women courageously face themselves and find it within themselves to understand, change, accept and finally love themselves. The choice to be loved by a truly loving new man stems from this inner journey.

Sometimes women who leave abusive relationships jump into a new one too fast because they are afraid they may not find anyone else again or they are afraid of being alone. This usually causes problems, because the time needed to explore themselves and to heal is not taken. Loneliness and depression are frightening things to have to deal with. It's not easy. Anger, disappointment, humiliation, regret, shame and other disturbing emotions and patterns need to be dealt with before a woman is healthy enough to sustain and accept a loving relationship with a new man. If you still have strong feelings for your previous mate and cannot get over the hate and anger you feel towards him, you are not ready. If you have feelings of worthlessness, desperation, fear, self-hate or even an absence of any emotions at all, you have not yet recovered.

To recover you need these primary things:
- Money

- Therapy

- Support in the form of friends/family/love

- Medical care

Your healing and recovery depend on your ability to build a life that is pleasurable and satisfying, and it is very hard to do that alone. It is also important to do things that interest you, such as mountain climbing or advancing your career. Healing does not mean just going into therapy or isolating yourself until you feel better. It means having the courage and the wisdom to reach out to a variety of experiences that life has to offer.

Surviving Depression

The pain of living in this world can sometimes be too much for some of us. Divorce, violence, poverty and an endless array of day-to-day problems can certainly lead one to question the value of one's life. Survivors of abuse very often grapple with depression and thoughts of suicide. That is understandable. What some people do not understand, however, is that these feelings are transitory. Time, therapy, support and a new, positive environment can alleviate these emotions.

"If only he had not been violent, if only he stopped hurting me," was the sentence that ran through my mind after I left the abusive man in my life and found myself alone in my very own apartment. I had made it that far. "We could have been together, I didn't have to leave if only..." For reasons I still do not understand, he would not stop his abusive behavior and I had to leave to save my mental and physical health. I had to let the dream go and I could not go back. I did not want to go back but at the same time, felt a very terrible sense of loss.

During my struggle to leave this relationship, there was help for me from women in support groups, shelters and therapists. With their help I was able to set myself up and get a new start. I fought, cried, kicked and screamed and got my way. I freed myself from him.

And then I was alone...

I felt a strange desire to end my life. I felt empty, alienated and tortured by the question, "What am I living for?" What was it to attain wealth, freedom, superb health and knowledge, and be all alone? I had no close ties, no one to love.

So I contemplated ending my own life. These thoughts were accompanied by a feeling of hopelessness, a loss of will to carry on. I contemplated suicide many times over the next few months.

There's not much one can say about dying. It's simply the end of life on earth. What I did was ride with it. I did not seek therapy, nor did I call anyone. Once in a while I would feebly mention it to someone in my support group, but I did not emphasize it. I did not act on my thoughts of death. I suffered through the feelings and hung on. My special friend, a Siamese cat that had been with me for ten years, often pulled me out of it. I just couldn't see how I could leave her. That was always a problem. I loved her so.

What I began to notice throughout this experience was that the feelings of depression and suicide ebbed within me like the flow of the tide. They came...and they went. And I discovered why.

My diet and vitamin intake (or deficiency) affected my emotions. Not eating properly definitely caused mood swings. (I began to gulp down a lot of vitamins—with instructions from carefully-researched books.) The other factor was thoughts. A song could throw me into the depths of misery. A change of attitude about my work could lift me to the sky. A preoccupation such as learning how to cook something new, totally blocked out any negative thoughts. It may sound humorous to say that cooking stopped my suicidal tendencies, but there is something to be learned here. Depression and suicidal tendencies come from a thought pattern, an attitude, a turning of the mind upon subjects that depress and cause a reaction. (Thoughts that are negative also cause an acid to flow through the body, I learned, while positive thoughts create protein.)

One does not necessarily need people (God bless them), I discovered, but one does need one's mind. Thoughts need to be directed towards hope, life and purpose... and food.

Change your thoughts and your feelings will change. Change your diet and you will feel better. Change your emotions and your reality changes. Thought accompanied by emotion manifests into reality.

After my own experience, I cannot stress enough the value of therapy, diet and exercise someone to talk to. It was a dangerous time for me and I was fortunate that I pulled myself out. But if ever these feelings came back, I would now immediately seek help. Why? Because it speeds things up and it helps enormously. Therapy also aids in detecting one's thought pattern that may take a long time to decipher alone.

Remember, depression will pass. Hold on and listen ever so carefully to your thoughts. They are the creators of your reality.

GO ON!

When you come to the Red Sea place in your life
When in spite of all you can do there is no way
  'round, there is no way back
There is now way BUT THROUGH
Then know God with a soul serene
And the dark and storm are gone
God stills the wind
God stills the waves
God says to your soul, "Go on! Go on!"

From *Life and Teaching of the Masters of the Far East*
Baird T. Spalding
(Devorss and Company, Marina Del Rey, California).
Reprinted by permission.

Chapter 13

Creating A New Reality

It has been said many times that what you think you are, you become. If you think negatively, you will create that negativity. If you think you cannot get out of an abusive relationship, that will become your reality. If you think you deserve no better than this abuser, so be it, you will never get anyone who treats you better. It is true, thoughts create the events and quality of your life.

But you must understand that it is not thoughts alone, as so many will have you believe, that are responsible for this. It is your feelings, caused by your thoughts, that do the manifesting.

No amount of positive thinking will change anything unless you have the feel of it. Words are empty without emotion. Nothing will happen. You cannot sit there and say, "I am valuable," and expect people to treat you that way, unless *you feel* it. It's not what you say that people react to, but what you feel about yourself. You have to *become* the word "valuable" in emotion before people will treat you as such.

If you think you are trapped in a destructive relationship, check out your emotions. You will have a feeling of hopelessness and helplessness that accompany your thoughts. This is what creates your reality.

I tried positive thinking for years along with visualization, but it never worked and I got very tired of it. It wasn't until I learned to concentrate on the emotion something gave me that my life began to change.

The most simple exercise I know is to meditate and visualize what it is you desire. When you see the picture and say the words, concentrate on the joyous feeling you get. Embrace it. Feel it. Become it. See yourself being loved in the way you want and feel it. Hold onto the feeling. Then release it. Bring it back as often as you can during your waking hours and feel it before you fall asleep and when you wake up. It will then manifest. Don't let anything get in the way of this exercise—no negative thoughts that produce negative emotion; no focusing on the opposite. Ignore those things. Ignore those who say it is not possible or that you can't have it. Stay on course. Never let it go.

We are all born with a healthy ego and it is never lost. Somewhere inside of us there is a place where we love ourselves in a natural way. That part of us knows without a doubt what loving behavior is. It desires to live in peace and joy and to express ourselves as we truly are. This place within each of us has been layered over with society's beliefs, attitudes and judgments as well as our own childhood programming. If you look for it, you will find it. You find it by becoming very quiet and aware of every emotion you have. It will speak to you. Ask it a question, and it will answer you. You do not need books, people or therapists to hear it, though they can help. It is yours alone and it will never fail you. Trust it. It is, in essence, you. The real you. Many will tell you it is the God part of you or the part of you that reaches God. Whatever your belief, hear it and heed it. No human being can give you the love that you find here.

The most important thing I have learned through the years is to think for myself and to be kind to me. I am the best friend I have and the one I ultimately listen to. During my search for happiness and the struggle to understand my unhappiness, I exposed myself to so much information, opinions and advice, I did not know whether I was coming or going.

In support groups I was told one thing, in books yet another. Therapists proclaimed me as a victim, a battered woman, an addict, and someone with a disease. Every answer to a simple question was complicated. And if I dared to sputter out any resistance to the labels and interpretations of my downfall of loving a jerk, I was immediately berated. "You are a victim. You have been victimized all your life. You have low self-esteem. You don't love yourself..." and on it went.

I arrived at the point where I threw out what everyone else had to say and asked myself. I asked simple questions and received simple answers. My mind and my feelings are my own. And, though it is true there are some who can help me identify myself and my behavior, no one can tell me what I am or why I do things except for myself.

Here are some of the things I concluded:

- Abusive men need women to abuse. If women remove their bodies from these men, make themselves inaccessible, we would not have any abusers in this entire country. To stop abuse, remove your body.

- If every abused woman in this country was given a cash gift of $100,000.00, the numbers of women in abusive relationships would drop immediately and drastically.

- If women were taught the signs of abuse early in grade school and it was provided as a mandatory class, little girls would grow up to be smart women. As a result, men would have to change because they would not be able to get a life partner.

- If every woman taught her son how to love himself we would have a world of loving men.

- There can by no tyrants unless there are victims.

- There can be no victims unless there are tyrants.

- If men had their jobs taken away as punishment for physically assaulting their partners instead of a small jail sentence, or were ordered to pay a hefty sum of money, almost all women would be safe.

Though it might be possible for some of these simple things to done in our society to prevent men from abusing women, societies do not often seem to have the capacity to think so simply or directly. We must, therefore, learn to do what we can ourselves.

Remove your body from your abuser. Love your son so he learns to love himself. Never be a victim by never being around a tyrant. Learn to get your own money. Educate yourself and your daughters, and do not expose them to a single harsh man. Never take a man's money into consideration when you are considering him for your life's partner.

Hard, you say? Can't be that simple?

Why complicate it?

Just for a moment, simplify it. It is a different perspective. You just might be able to see the beauty of simplicity, a long-lost art.

EPILOGUE

"You can thank O.J. Simpson for that. Very timely," a new acquaintance responded when I told her about the exciting news that this book was about to be published and distributed nationally. I was taken aback by her casual comment.

The day I thank O.J. Simpson for having anything to do with this book is a day that will never meet the dawn. As for timely, the message in it has been struggling to be heard for well over two years, just as millions of women in this country have been crying out for decades. The devastating problem of domestic violence has long been with us, it's just that few talked about it and even fewer wrote about it until about ten years ago. It is sad that it took the tragedy of O.J. Simpson to compel our country to take a new look at the bruised face of domestic relations. It was he, after all, who so terrorized his wife Nicole, her gut wrenching sobs for help echoing across the nation for all of us to hear on the 911 call to Los Angeles police taped in 1989. Every abused woman who heard it could identify with the sheer desperation in her plea. For men, it was an embarrassment. Spousal battery was not something of which a national football star, a truly "good guy" was supposed to be guilty, at least not publicly. Behind closed doors, well, that might be another matter.

Please Don't Let Him Hurt Me Anymore

Although for about three weeks after the Simpson tragedy surfaced, crisis lines for battered women rang off the walls across the country, and lawmakers scrambled to push new bill on domestic violence through state legislatures, it wasn't long before Nicole Simpson's voice faded into the background. With an astonishing 3,500 letters pouring into O.J. Simpson's prison per day, and with viewers in the millions glued to their televisions for the latest news, it is clear that our collective consciousness is obsessed with the man, O.J. Simpson, not the issue of domestic violence. We are fascinated by this broken man, once a revered football star, wealthy, famous and free, now accused of the murder of his ex-wife and her young male friend. Why this obsession? Because we are outraged by his violent physical and verbal abuse of his ex-wife? No. We are fascinated by fame, fortune and murder. We are intrigued with the possibility he may be guilty, probably the most famous accused murder suspect in American history. It was only when he became a murder suspect, not simply a batterer that he became the object of our rapt attention. I find that fact frightening and wonder what it says about our society.

It appears Americans have a casual view of violence towards women. We downplay the issue of spousal abuse, brushing it off as "everyone goes through this. It's normal. It's forgivable." Domestic violence could not exist to such an extent if we did not share the attitude reflected in the televised comment of a bystander at the courthouse where Simpson was being arraigned. "I'm at the point where I like the guy so much, I don't care what he did." From the looks of it, so do countless others.

Domestic violence is not going to go away after the Simpson trial is over. Men will continue to display violent behavior toward the women who love them. Though the media will not cover a great many of these incidents, women will continue to run, hide and seek shelter. They will go on suffering, living lives of terror.

EPILOGUE

Until we as a society, as a whole, insist that this is not acceptable, that it is wrong and a violation, it will continue. The results of this ongoing violence will be felt by all of us in many ways if we do not stop it. It effects our economy, our mental and physical health, and, most of all, it effects our children who will grow up to carry on the tradition, stronger in numbers, more violent than their parents. There will be more crime, more pain, more lives snuffed out. More women will stop working and more will commit suicide. Love will be the victim as domestic violence continues to crack the foundation of our society. No one, but no one is spared.

I know I speak for many women I say that we long to go home and sleep peacefully in the arms of the men we love. We want them to be our partners, not our enemies. We need them on our side, to respect and care for us as we do for them. We want our men to love our children and yes, even the family pet. We want them to teach our offspring what it means for a man to love a woman and how powerful and joyous that union can be. We are standing at the brink of great world changes, and we want our men to face the future courageously with us. We want to go home at the end of the day, not flee to shelters and safe houses or take to the streets in terror for our lives and those of our children. We want to slumber in our own beds, not in cars. We do not want to accept poverty as a welcome alternative to being beaten and brutalized in our houses. We want to be loved. We want to be safe. Dear God, let us go home.

We don't want to shatter the night again and again with our cries of pain and pleas for help, calling out for all to hear, "Please don't let him hurt me anymore."

Alexis Asher
Los Angeles, July, 1984

177

LAUGHTER

In spite of the seriousness and painful subject matter of this book, I feel it mportant for me to close it with a comment about the ability to laugh.

Laughter...I heard it in shrieks. I saw women laughing so hard the tears rolled down their cheeks. In support groups, counseling clinics and shelters, between the tears, they laughed. Apart from the women I met who were abused, only their therapists could top them. I never met a more genuinely lighthearted group than these professionals.

Today, I understand that without this ability to laugh, there would be no recovery.

And now, when they laugh...I laugh with them.

Resources

The numbers listed on the following pages will put you in touch with coalition organizations, shelters or safe houses, childrens protective services and legal, medical, financial and security services in your locality. Many provide 24-hour crisis counseling by telephone and often accept collect calls. These are vital information and referral sources. They can direct you to non-resident support groups, counseling and advocacy services and countless agencies and organizations that offer battered women and their children help in all needs. Coalitions, resource centers, women's centers, legal aid, military family centers, programs for men who batter and therapy are just some of the things they can help you with. Do not be afraid to call, or ask questions.

The listings are organized under these headings:

CHILDREN'S SERVICES

Children's services can help you obtain day care, child support and protection for your children.

COALITIONS

Coalitions can refer you to the domestic violence program and shelter in your area.

LEGAL

Legal services can provide referrals to attorneys who specialize in family law and can provide legal assistance help you protect your rights.

MEDICAL/HEALTH

These services can help you find medical care when you need it.

MONEY

The services listed under this heading can help refer you to community resources that may be able to offer financial assistance or that can help you obtain compensation if you are the victim of a crime.

PERSONAL SAFETY

Resources that can help teach you self-defense or provide security services for you.

PROGRAMS FOR MEN WHO BATTER

Resources that help men deal with their propensity towards violence.

NOTE: Every effort has been made to ensure that the information contained in these pages was accurate at the time of publication. However, due to the voluntary nature of many of these organizations, and the problems of coordinating funding and staffing, it is possible that some of these services may not be active when you read this book. The vast majority, however, are stable and well established. All of the telephone numbers were in service in July, 1994, and were verified by personal contact by the author. Telephone numbers may change every so often, but they are usually listed so you should be able to call Information for the new one. You can also call a service in another town or city and ask for a local referral, or call one of the numbers listed in the "National" section beginning on page 326 for help. The author and publisher welcome new and revised listing information. Please send such information to the attention of the author at the publisher's address listed on the copyright page of this book.

ALABAMA

CHILDREN
Child Abuse Reporting Hotline
c/o Department of Human Resources
3030 Mobile Highway
Montgomery, AL 36108
(205) 293-310

State Line
(205) 242-9500

Child Support Enforcement
Montgomery
(205) 242-9300

COALITIONS
Alabama Coalition Against Domestic Violence
P.O. Box 4762
Montgomery, AL 36101
Contact person: Carol Gundlach
(205) 832-4842

LEGAL
State Bar of Alabama
P. O. Box 671
Montgomer, AL 35101
(205) 269-1515

MONEY
Crime Victim Compensation
P. O. Box 1548
Montgomery, AL 36102

PERSONAL SAFETY
State Attorney General's Office
Montgomery, AL
(205) 242-7300
For information on state stalking laws.

PROGRAMS FOR MEN WHO BATTER
Riverbend
635 West College Street
P. O. Box 941
Florence, AL 35631
(205) 764-3431

SHELTERS AND SAFE HOUSES

ANNISTON
The Salvation Army's Women's Shelter
(205) 236-5644

AUBURN
E.A.T.F.B.W.
(205) 887-9330

BIRMINGHAM
Family Violence Project
(2015) 792-3603

COLUMBIA
SAFE House of Shelby County
(205) 669-1320

DOTHAN
House of Ruth
(205) 792-3603

FLORENCE
Safeplace Crisis Line
(205) 767-6210

GADSEN
The Shelter
(205) 543-3059

HUNTSVILLE
H.O.P.E. Place Crisis Line
(205) 539-3434

MOBILE
Penelope House Crisis Line
(205) 432-1730

JASPER
Daybreak/Family Resource Center of NW Alabama
(205) 387-1186

MONTGOMERY
Mongomery Area Family Violence Program
(205) 263-0218

PHOENIX CITY
Russell County Shelter for Battered Women
(205) 297-4401

SELMA
Black Belt Regional Domestic Violence Program
(205) 874-8711

TUSCALOOSA
Spouse Abuse Network
(205) 758-0808

ALASKA

COALITIONS
Alaska Network on Domestic Violence and Sexual
Assault
419 6th Street #116
Juneau, AK 99801
Contact person: Cindy Smith
(907)586-3650

SHELTERS AND SAFE HOUSES

ANCHORAGE
AWAKE
(907) 272-0100

BARROW
Arctic Women in Crisis
(907) 852-4357

BETHEL
Tundra Women's Coalition
(907) 543-3456

DILLINGHAM
SAFE
(907) 842-2316

EMMONAK
Emmonak Women's Shelter
(907) 949-1434

FAIRBANKS
Women In Crisis
(907) 452-2293

HOMER
South Peninsula Women's Services
(907) 235-8101

JUNEAU
Alaska Network on Domestic Violence and Sexual
Assault
(907) 586-3650

AWARE
(907) 586-1090

Juneau Women's Resource Center
(907) 586-2977

KENAI
Lee Shore Women's Resource Center
(907) 283-7257

KETCHIKAN
Women In Safe Homes
(907) 225-9474

KODIAK
Kodiak Women's Resource and Crisis Center
(907) 486-3625

KOTZEBUE
Kotzebue Women's Crisis Project
(907) 442-3969

NOME
Bering Sea Women's Group
(907) 443-5444

PALMER
Valley Women's Resource Center
(907) 746-4080

SITKA
Sitkans Against Family Violence
(607) 747-33705

UNALASKA
Unalaskans Against Sexual Assault and Family Violence
(607) 581-1500

VALDEZ
Advocates for victims of Violence
(907) 835-2999

WASILLA
Valley Women's Resource Center
(607) 376-4080

ARIZONA

CHILDREN
Child Abuse Reporting Hotline
Phoenix
(602) 266-0282

Child Support Enforcement
15 South 15th Avenue
Phoenix, AZ 85007
(602) 258-1473

COALITIONS
Arizona Coalition Against Domestic Violence
100 W. Camelback #109
Phoenix, AZ 85013
Contact person: Sharon Ersch
(602) 279-2900

LEGAL
Arizona Bar Center
111 West Monroe, Suite 1800
Phoenix, AZ 85003
(602) 252-4804

MONEY
Victim Compensation Bureau
301 West Jefferson, 7th Floor
Phoenix, AZ 85003
(602) 506-4955

PERSONAL SAFETY
State Attorney General's Office
1275 West Washington
Phoenix, AZ 85007
(602) 542-5025

186

PROGRAMS FOR MEN WHO BATTER

Family Counseling Agency
209 South Tuscon Blvd., Suite F
Tucson, AZ 85716
(602) 327-4583

SHELTERS AND SAFE HOUSES

CASA GRANDE
Against Abuse
(602) 836-0858

CHANDLER
My Sister's Place
(602) 821-1024

COTTONWOOD
Catholic Social Services Family Violence Hotline
(602) 634-4524

FLAGSTAFF
Flagstaff Battered Women's Shelter
(602) 774-7353

GLENDALE
Faith House
(602) 939-6798

KINGMAN
Kingman Association for Abused Persons
(602) 753-4242

MESA
Autumn House
(602) 835-5555

MIAMI
The Caring Place Advocate House
(602) 473-3752

NOGALES
Domestic Violence Program
(602) 281-2440

PHOENIX
De Colores
(602) 269-1515

Sojourn Center
(602) 258-5344

PRESCOTT
Faith House
(602) 445-4673

SCOTTSDALE
Chrysalis/Sunnyslope
(602) 481-0402

SIERRA VISTA
Domestic Violence Crisis Shelter
(602) 458-9096

TEMPE
Arizona Coalition Against Domestic Violence/Autumn
House
(602) 831- 5022

TUSCON
AVA Crisis Shelter
(602) 795-4880

Brewster Crisis Shelter Services
(602) 622-6347

Tuscon Shelter for Women and Children
(602) 795-4266

YUMA
Safe House
(602) 782-0044

ARKANSAS

COALITIONS
Arkansas Coalition Against Violence To Women &
Children
7509 Cantrell Road #213
Little Rock, AR 72207
Contact person: Schatzi Riley
(501) 663-4668

LEGAL
State Bar Association
Little Rock
(501) 663-4668

PROGRAMS FOR MEN WHO BATTER
STATE INFORMATION LINE
(800) 332-4443
    Ask for a referral for programs for men. Also will
help with other domestic violence concerns.

SHELTERS AND SAFE HOUSES

ARKADELPHIA
Domestic Violence Project
(501) 246-2587

BATESVILLE
Family Violence Prevention
(501) 793-4011

CAMDEN
Women's Crisis Center
(501) 836-8272

HARRISON
Sanctuary
(501) 741-2121

LITTLE ROCK
Advocates for Battered Women
(501) 376-3219

PINE BLUFF
CASA Women's Shelter
(501) 535-0287

RUSSELLVILLE
River Valley Shelter for Women
(501) 968-3110

TEXARKANA
Domestic Violence Prevention, Inc.
(501) 773-5858

CALIFORNIA

CHILDREN

LOS ANGELES
Los Angeles County Child Abuse Hotline
(800) 540-4000

Crystal Stairs, Inc.
(213) 299-1199
　　Will refer you to a daycare center in your area. Resources, subsidized programs, federally funded child care food programs for licensed child care providers and research.

SACRAMENTO
Office of Child Support
(916) 654-1532
　　State office for women who need help collecting child support.

State Department of Justice Central Registry
(916) 227-3593
    Call for information in your area to help you collect child support.

SAN DIEGO
San Diego Children's Services Bureau and Abuse Reporting Hotline
(619) 650-2191

SAN FRANCISCO
San Francisco and County Child Abuse Reporting Hotline
(415) 431-5133

COALITIONS
Northern California Coalition for Battered Women and Children
1717 5th Avenue
San Rafael, CA 94901
Contact person: Donna Garske
(415) 457-2464

Southern California Coalition For Battered Women
P.O. Box 5036
Santa Monica, California 90409
(213) 655-6098

LEGAL
State Bar of California
555 Franklin Street
San Francisco, California 94102
(415) 561-8200
    Call and they will refer you to legal organizations in your city which specialize in helping women who are victims of domestic violence.

MEDICAL/HEALTH

AIDS Hotline
800-922-AIDS

Plane Tree Health Resource Center
2300 California Street Suite 201
San Francisco, California 94115
(415) 923-3680
(415) 923-3681
    Helpline for resources and information. Can help you pick a physician and and connect you to women who have similar health problems as you., including effects of abuse. Talk, read and learn about medical care and your health.

Medicare and Social Security
800-772-1213

MONEY

State Board of Control Victim of Crime Program
800-777-9229
(916) 322-4426
    Referrals to community resources. Crisis intervention. Victim of crime financial compensation and court support services.

PERSONAL SAFETY

Model Mugging
801 Lighthouse Avenue
Monterey, California 93940
(408) 659-2041
    Contact them for a program near you. Teaches self-defense in situations of rape or mugging. Includes marital rape.

PROGRAMS FOR MEN WHO BATTER

ENCINO
Alternatives to Violence Program
(818) 986-9964

OAKLAND
Oakland Men's Project
(510) 835-2433

SACRAMENTO
ALIVE
Positive Anger Control
(916) 920-2952 Hotline
(916) 448-2321 Office

SAN DIEGO AND AREA
YWCA General Counseling Services
(619) 270-4504

SHELTERS AND SAFE HOUSES

ANTELOPE VALLEY
Valley Oasis
(805) 945-6736
M-F, limited Spanish.

ARTESIA
SuCa Family Crisis and Support Center
(213) 402-4888

AUBURN
Placer Women's Center
(916) 652-6558

BAKERSFIELD
Alliance On Family Violence
(805) 327-1091

BARSTOW
Desert Sanctuary
(619) 252-3441

BELMONT
San Mateo Battered Women's Shervices
(415) 312-8515

BIG BEAR LAKE
Doves
(909) 866-5723

CAMARILLO
Interface Community Ark
(805) 496-1994

CARSON
Carson Shelter
(310) 549-1375

CLAREMONT
House Of Ruth
(909) 988-5559

COLTON
Option House
(909) 381-3471

DAVIS
Harper House
(916) 371-1907

EAST LOS ANGELES
East Los Angeles Shelter
(213) 268-7564
Spanish available.

EL CENTRO
Woman Haven Inc.
(619) 353-8530

FORT BRAGG
Project Sanctuary
(707) 964-4357

FREMONT
SAVE
(510) 794-6055

FRENCH CAMP
Haven of Peace
(209) 982-0396

FRESNO
YWCA Marjaree Mason Center
(209) 237-4701

GLENDALE
Glendale YWCA Shelter
(818) 242-1106
This shelter is called a "Phase Two" shelter and accommodates women for up to six months. Help in finding permanent housing, educational classes, financial planning, groups, therapy and resources for children are all part of the program.
Only available to women who have already been in another shelter for abused women.

HAYWARD
Emergency Shelter Program
(510) 449-786-1246

HERMOSA BEACH
1736 Family Crisis Center
(310) 379-3620

HIGHLAND
Bethlehem House
(714) 862-8027
24 hour Spanish available.

JOSHUA TREE
Morongo Basin Unity Home
(619) 366-9663

LAGUNA
Human Options
(714) 494-5367

LAKEWOOD/CERRITOS
Su Casa
(310) 402-7081
(310) 402-4888
Spanish available.

LONG BEACH
YWCA Women's Shelter
(310) 437-4663

LOS ANGELES
Good Shepherd Shelter
(213) 737-6111

LOS ANGELES (SOUTH CENTRAL)
Jenesse Center
(213) 751-1145

Free Spirit Shelter
(213) 937-1312

MODESTO
Haven Women's Center
(209) 577-5980

MONTEREY
YWCA of Monterey Peninsula
(408) 372-6300

MOUNTAINVIEW
Mid-Peninsula Support Network
(415) 940-7855

NEWARK
Second Chance Emergency Shelter
(510) 792-4357

NEWBURY PARK
Interface Community
(805) 496-1994

NEWHALL
Association to Aid Victims of Domestic Violence
(805) 259-8175

OAKLAND
A Safe Place
(510) 536-7233

Battered Women's Alternatives
(510) 930-8300

Oceanside
Woman's Resource Center
(619) 757-3500

ORANGE
Women's Transitional Living Center
(714) 992-1932

PASADENA
Haven House
(213) 681-2626

PINE GROVE
Operation Care
(209) 223-2600

PLACERVILLE
El Dorado Women's Center
(916) 626-1131

REDDING
Shasta County Women's Refuge
(916) 244-01117

RIVERSIDE
Horizon House
(909) 683-0829

SACRAMENTO
W.E.A.V.E., Inc.
(916) 920-2952

SALINAS
Family Emergency Shelter
(408) 422-2201

SAN ANDREAS
Calaveras Women's Crisis Line
(209) 736-4011

SAN DIEGO
Battered Women's Services
(619) 234-3164

SAN FERNANDO VALLEY
Haven Hills
(818) 887-6589

SAN FRANCISCO
La Casa De Las Madres
(415) 333-1515

Rosalie House
(415) 255-0165

Woman, Inc.
(415) 864-4722

SAN JOSE
Next Door
(408) 279-2962

SAN LIUS OBISPO
Women's Shelter Program
(805) 544-6163

SAN MATEO
Battered Women's Services
(415) 312-8515

Northern California Shelter Support Services
(415) 342-0850

SAN PEDRO
Rainbow Services
(310) 547-9343

SAN RAFAEL
Marin Abused Women Services
(415) 924-3456

SANTA BARBARA
Santa Barbara Shelter
(805) 964-5245

SANTA MARIA
Shelter Services for Women, Inc.
(805) 925-2160

SANTA MONICA
Sojourn
(310) 392-9896

SANTA ROSA
YWCA Women's Emergency Shelter Program
(707) 546-1234

SEAL BEACH
Interval House
(310) 594-4555

SONORA
Mother Lode Women's Crisis Center
(209) 532-4707

SOUTH LAKE TAHOE
South Lake Tahoe Women's Center
(916) 544-4444

SUSANVILLE
Lassen Family Services, Inc.
(916) 257-5004

Please Don't Let Him Hurt Me Anymore

VENTURA
Ventura County Coalition Against Household Violence
(805) 656-1111

VICTORVILLE
High Desert Domestic Violence Hotline
(619) 242-9179

VISALIA
Family Services of Tulare County
(209) 732-5941

WEST COVINA
YWCA Wings
(818) 967-0658

WEST HOLLYWOOD
Everywoman's Shelter
(213) 653-4042
     Available to those of Chinese, Japanese, Korean, Philipino and Vietnamese nationalities.

WHITTIER
Women and Children's Crisis Shelter
(310) 945-3939 (24-hour)

YREKA
Siskiyou Domestic Violence Program
(916) 842-4068

YUBA CITY
Casa de Esperanza
(916) 674-2040

COLORADO

COALITIONS
Colorado Domestic Violence Coalition
P.O. Box 18902
Denver, CO 80218
Contact person: Jan McKish
(303) 573-9018

LEGAL
Colorado State Bar Association
Denver
(303) 860 1112

PROGRAMS FOR MEN WHO BATTER
Alternatives to Family Violence
Northglen
(303) 450-6161

AMEND and Cherokee Counseling
Denver
(303) 832-6363

Options in Non-Violence
Fort Collins
(303) 221-0582

SHELTERS AND SAFE HOUSES
ARVADA
Women In Crisis
(303) 420-6757

ASPEN
Response
(303) 920-5347

AURORA
Gateway Battered Women's Shelter
(303) 343-1851

BOULDER
Boulder County Safehouse
(303) 449-8623

Domestic Violence Prevention Center
(303) 633-3819

Women's Shelter
(303) 441-4444

CANON CITY
Family Crisis Services, Inc.
(719) 275-2429

CASTLE ROCK
Women's Crisis Center of Douglas County
(303) 688-8484

COLORADO SPRINGS
Domestic Violence Prevention Center
(719) 633-3819

COMMERCE CITY
Canyon City Family Crisis Center
(303) 289-4441

CRAIG
Abused and Battered Humans
(303) 824-2400

DENVER
Brandon Center
(303) 620-9190

Safe House For Battered Women
(303) 830-6800

Servicios De La Raza
(303) 458-7088

DURANGO
Alternative Horizons
(303) 247-9619

Volunteers of America Southwest Safehouse
(303) 259-5443

FORT COLLINS
Crossroads
(303) 482-3502

FORT MORGAN
S.H.A.R.E.
(303) 867-3411

GLENWOOD SPRINGS
Family Violence Assistance Program
(303) 945-3939

GRAND JUNCTION
Domestic Violence Project
(303) 241- 6704

GREELEY
A Woman's Place
(303) 356-4226

LONGMONT
Longmont Coalition for Women in Crisis
(303) 772-4422

LOVELAND
Alternatives For Battered Women
(303) 669-5150

MEEKER
Safehouse, Inc.
(303) 878-3131

MONTROSE
Women's Resource Center
(303) 249-2486

PUEBLO
YWCA Family Crisis Shelter
(303) 545-8195

SALIDA
Alliance Against Domestic Violence
(719) 539-2596

STEAMBOAT SPRINGS
Advocates Against Battering and Abuse
(303) 879-8888

TRINIDAD
Together in Friendship
(303) 846-HELP

VAIL
Women' s Resource Center of Eagle County
(303) 476-7384

YUMA
Yuma Community Resource Center/New Directions
(303) 848-5441

CONNECTICUT

COALITIONS
Connecticut Coalition Against Domestic Violence
135 Broad Street
Hartford, CT 06105
Contact person: Anne Menard
(203) 524-5890

LEGAL

Connecticut State Bar Association
Rocky Hill
(203) 721-0025

PROGRAMS FOR MEN WHO BATTER

Men And Stress Control
YMCA
651 State Street
Bridgeport 06604
(203) 334-5551

    The Connecticut Coalition Against Domestic Violence can also refer you to more programs for men who are abusive in your area.

SHELTERS AND SAFE HOUSES

ARSONIA
The Umbrella Project
(203) 736-994

BRIDGEPORT
Bridgeport YWCA Shelter Services For Abused Families
(203) 333-7555

DAYVILLE
Domestic Violence Program of United Services Inc.
(203) 456-9476

GREENWICH
Greenwich YWCA Domestic Abuse Services
(203) 622-0003

HARTFORD
Connecticut Coalition On Abused Women
(203) 524-5890
Interval House
(203) 527-0550

MERIDIAN
Meridian-Wallingford Chrysalis
(203) 238-1501

MIDDLETOWN
New Horizons
(203) 347-6971

NEW BRITAIN
Prudence Crandall Center for Women
(203) 225-6357

NEW HAVEN
New Haven Project for Battered women
(203) 789-8104

NEW LONDON
Genesis House/Women's Center
(203) 447-0366

NORWALK
Women's Crisis Center
(203) 852-1980

SHARON
Women's Emergency Services
(203) 824-1880

STAMFORD
Stamford Domestic Violence Services, Inc.
(203) 357-8162

SOUTH NORWALK
Women's Crisis Center, A Member of the Safe Home
Network
(203) 852-1980

TORRINGTON
Susan B. Anthony Project For Women
(203) 482-7133

WATERBURY
Women's Emergency Shelter
(203) 575-0036

DELAWARE

COALITIONS

Delaware Coalition Against Domestic Violence
c/o Child Inc.
507 Philadelphia Pike
Wilmington, DE 19809
Contact person: Mary Davis
(302) 762-6110

LEGAL

Delaware State Bar Association
Wilmington
(302) 658-5278

PROGRAMS FOR MEN WHO BATTER

Parents Anonymous of Delaware Inc.
124-D Senatorial Drive
Wilmington, Delaware 19807
(302) 654-1102
    Will refer you to programs for abusers.

SHELTERS AND SAFE HOUSES

MILFORD
Families In Transition Center/People's Place 11, Inc.
(302) 422-8058

WILMINGTON
CHILD, Inc./Family Violence Program
(302) 762-6110

DISTRICT OF COLUMBIA

COALITIONS

D. C. Coalition Against Domestic Violence
P. O. Box 76069
Washington, DC 20013
Contact person: Donna Edwards
(202) 783-5332

SHELTERS AND SAFE HOUSES

WASHINGTON
House of Ruth/Herspace
(202) 347-2777

WASHINGTON
My Sister's Place
(202) 529-5991

FLORIDA

CHILDREN

Florida Abuse Hotline
(800) 342-9152

COALITIONS

Florida Coalition Against Domestic Violence
P. O. Box 1201
Winter Park, FL 32790
Contact person: Sue Peterson Armstrong
(904) 377-5690

LEGAL

Florida Bar Association
Tallahassee
(904) 561-5600

PROGRAMS FOR MEN WHO BATTER

Advocates Program
1515 NW 7th Street, #112
Miami, FL 33125
(305) 649-8422
        Provides local and statewide programs for men who are abusive.

SHELTERS AND SAFE HOUSES

BARTOW
Peace River Center
(813) 533-3141

BRADENTON
Hope Family Services Inc.
(813) 755-6805

BUNNELL
Family Life Center
(904) 437-3505

CLEARWATER
Spouse Abuse Shelter of RCS
(813) 344-5555

COCOA
The Salvation Army Domestic Violence Shelter
(407) 631-2764

DAYTONA BEACH
Domestic Abuse Council
(904) 255-2102

DELRAY BEACH
Aid to victims of Domestic Assault Inc.
(407) 265-2900

FORT LAUDERDALE
Women in Distress
(305) 761-1133

Please Don't Let Him Hurt Me Anymore

FORT MYERS
Abuse Counseling and Treatment Inc.
(813) 939-3112

GAINESVILLE
Sexual and Physcial Abuse Resource Center
(904) 377-8255

INVERNESS
CASA/Citrus Abuse Shelter Association Inc.
(904) 344-8111

JACKONSVILLE
Hubbard House
(904) 354-3114

KISSIMMEE
Help NOW
(407) 847-8811

LAKELAND
Peace River Center
(813) 682-7270

LEESBURG
Haven, Inc.
(904) 753-5800

MARATHON
Domestic Abuse Shelter Inc.
(305) 743-4440

MIAMI
Metro-Dade Advocates for Victims
(305) 758-2546

OCALA
Ocala Rape Crisis/Spouse Abuse Center
(904) 622-8495

ORLANDO
Spouse Abuse Inc.
(407) 886-2856

PENSACOLA
Favor House
(904) 434-6600

PANAMA CITY
The Salvation Army Domestic Violence Program
(904) 763-0706

PORT CHARLOTTE
C.A.R.E.
(813) 627-6000

PUENTA GORDA
Center for Rape and Abuse Inc.
(813) 627-6000

SARASOTA
Safe Place and Rape Crisis Center
(813) 365-1976

SAINT PETERSBURG
Center Against Spouse Abuse
(813) 898-3671

TALLAHASSEE
Refuge House Inc.
(904) 681-2111

TAMPA
The Spring of Tampa Bay Inc.
(813) 247-7233

WEST PALM BEACH
Harmony House
(407) 655-6106

GEORGIA

COALITIONS
Georgia Advocates For Battered Women And Children
250 Georgia Avenue SE, #365
Atlanta 30312
Contact person: Suzannah Pogue
(404) 524-3847

LEGAL
Georgia State Bar Association
Atlanta
(404) 656-3490

PROGRAMS FOR MEN WHO BATTER

Men Stopping Violence, Inc.
1025 DeKalb Avenue, #25
Atlanta, GA 30307
(404) 688-1376
    Call for referrals in your area.

SHELTERS AND SAFE HOUSES

ALBANY
Liberty House
(912) 439-7065

ATHENS
Project Safe
(404) 543-3331

ATLANTA
Council on Battered Women
(404) 873-1766

AUGUSTA
Safe Homes of Augusta Inc.
(706) 736-2499

212

BLUE RIDGE
No. Georgia Mountain Crisis Network
(706) 632-8400

BRUNSWICK
Amity House
(912) 264-4357

CALHOUN
Calhoun/Gordon Council on Battered Women
(404) 629-1111

CARTERVILLE
Christian League for Battered Women
(404) 386-8779

CLARKSVILLE
Circle of Hope
(404) 776-3406

COLUMBUS
Columbus Alliance for Battered Women Inc.
(404) 324-3850

CUMMING
Family Haven
(404) 889-6384

DALTON
Northwest Georgia Family Crisis Center Inc.
(706) 278-5586

DECATUR
Women's Resource Center of Dekalb
(404) 688-9436

FORT BENNING
Army Family Advocay Program
(706) 545-2011

GAINSVILLE
Gateaway House
(404) 536-5860

Please Don't Let Him Hurt Me Anymore

HAINESVILLE
Tri-County Protective Agency
(912) 368-9200

LAGRANGE
Project of Love Inc.
(404) 882-1000

LEBANON
Cherokee Family Violence Center Inc.
(404) 479-1703

MACON
Macon Rescue Mission/Battered Women Division
(912) 750-0034

MARIETTA
YWCA of Cobb County/Crisis Intervention Department
(404) 427-3390

MORROW
Association on Battered Women of Clayton County
(404) 996-HELP

ROME
Hospitality House for Women Inc.
(404) 235-4673

SAVANNAH
S.A.F.P. Shelter Inc.
(912) 234-9999

TIFTON
Brother Charlie Rescue Center
(912) 386-0645

WARNER ROBINS
Salvation Army Safe House
(912) 923-6294

WAYCROSS
Waycross Shelter
(912) 285-5850

HAWAII

COALITIONS
Hawaii State Committee on Family Violence
2500 Pali Highway
Honolulu, HI 96817
(808) 595-3900

MONEY
Victim/Witness Assistance Program
Department of Prosecuting Attorney
200 High Street
Wailuku 96793
(808) 243-7777

LEGAL
Hawaii State Bar Association
Honolulu
(808) 537-1868

MONEY
Victim/Witness Assistance Program
Department of Prosecuting Attorney
200 High Street
Wailuku 96793
(808) 243-7777

PROGRAMS FOR MEN WHO BATTER
Alternatives To Violence
P.O. Box 909
Wailuku, HI 96793
(808) 242-9559

Alternatives To Violence
P.O. Box 10488
Hilo, HI 96721
(808) 969-7798

SHELTERS AND SAFE HOUSES

HILO
Family Crisis Center Inc.
(808) 959-8400

HONOLULU
Child and Family Shelter for Abused Spouses and
Children
(808) 841-0822

Military Family Abuse Shelter
(808) 533-7125

HOOLEHUA
Hale Laiku
(808) 567-6420

LIHUE
YWCA Family Violence Shelter
(808) 245-6362

MAUI
Women Helping Women
(808) 579-9581

OAHU
Shelter for Abused Spouses and Children
(808) 841-0822

IDAHO

COALITIONS
Idaho Network To Stop Violence Against Women
P.O. Box 714
Blackfoot, ID 83221
Contact person: Jo Hardin
(208) 785-1047

LEGAL
Idaho State Bar Association
Boise
(208) 334-4500

PROGRAMS FOR MEN WHO BATTER
Domestic Violence Crisis Line
Idaho Falls
(208) 525-1820
> Call for a referral.

ACAP
Boise
(208) 338-1323

SHELTERS AND SAFE HOUSES

AMERICAN FALLS
Power County Domestic Violence Support Group
(208) 226-2311

BLACKFOOT
Bingham Crisis Center for Women
(208) 785-1047

BOISE
Women's Crisis Center
(208) 343-7025

COEUR D'ALENE
Women's Center
(208) 664-1443 (Referral only)

LEWISTON
YWCA Lewsiton/Clarkston Crisis Services
(208) 746-9655

NAMPA
Mercy House
(208) 467-4130

TWIN FALLS
Volunteers Against Domestic Violence
(208) 733-0100

WALLACE
Shoshone County Women's Resource Center
(208) 556-6101

ILLINOIS

COALITIONS
Illinois Coalition Against Domestic Violence
937 South Fourth Street
Springfield, IL 62703
Contact person: Joyce M. Pruitt
(217) 789-2830

LEGAL
Illinois State Bar Association
Chicago
(312)-726-8775

PROGRAMS FOR MEN WHO BATTER
M.O.V.E.
Men Overcoming Violence
Chicago
(312) 327-0036
        Can refer you to other programs in Chicago or your area.

SHELTERS AND SAFE HOUSES

ALSTON
Oasis Women's Center
(618) 465-1978

BELLEVILLE
Women's Crisis Center of Metro East
(618) 235-0892

BLOOMINGTON
MId-central Community Action, Inc.
(309) 827- 7070

CAIRO
Community Health Services, Inc.
(618) 734-4357

CANTON
Fulton County Women's Crisis Service
(309) 647-8311

CARBONDALE
Women's Center
(618) 529-2324

CAIRO
Cairo's Women Center
(618) 734-HELP

CENTRALIA
People Against Violent Environments
(618) 533-7233

CHARLESTON
Coalition Against Domestic Violence
(217) 345-4300

CHICAGO
Chicago Abused Women Coalition/ Greenhouse Shelter
(312) 278-4566

Family Rescue
(312) 375-8400

Harriet Tubman Shelter
(312) 924-3152

Neopolitan LIghthouse
(312) 638-0227

Rainbow House/ Arco Iris
(312) 762-6611

Sarah's Inn
(708) 386-4225

St. Francis Shelter
(312) 236-5172

DANVILLE
YWCA Women's Shelter
(217) 443-5566

DEKALB SAFE PASSAGE INC.
(815) 756-5228

DECATUR
Dove Domestic Violence Program
(217) 423-2238

DES PLAINES
Life Span Inc.
(708) 824-4454

HARRISBURG
Anna Bixby Women's Center
(618) 252-8389

HAZELCREST
South Surburban Family Shelter, Inc.
(312) 335-4125

JACKSONVILLE
Womens's Crisis Center
(217) 243-4357

JOLIET
Groundwork Guardian Angel Home of Joliet
(815) 722-3344

KANKAKEE
Kankakee County Coalition
(815) 932-5800

LINCOLN
Logan County Committee Against Domestic Violence
and Sexual
(217) 732-7011

OLNEY
C.A.R.E.S./YWCA
(312) 748-5660

PEORIA
Tri County Women Strength
(309) 691-4111

PRINCETON
Freedom House
(815) 875-8233

QUINCY
Quincy Area Network Against Domestic Abuse
(217) 222-2873

ROCHELLE
Hope of Rochelle
(815) 562-8890

ROCK ISLAND
Christian Family Care Center
(309) 788-2273

ROCKFORD
P.H.A.S.E./W.A.V.E.
(815) 962-6102

SPRINGFIELD
Sojourn's Women's Center
(217) 544-2484

STERLING
COVE/YWCA
(815) 626-7277

STREATOR
Alternative to Domestic Violence
(800) 892-3375

URBANA
A Women's Fund/ A Women's Place
(217) 384-4390

WAUKEGAN
A Safe Place
(312) 249-4450

WOODSTOCK
Turning Point
(815) 338-8080

WYANET
Freedom House
(815) 875-8233

INDIANA

COALITIONS

Indiana Coalition Against Domestic Violence
P. O. Box 2048
Louisville, KY 40201
Contact person: Leslie Hammelman
(502) 581-7231

PROGRAMS FOR MEN WHO BATTER

Center For Non-Violence
235 West Creighton
Fort Wayne, IN 46802
(219) 456-4112

LEGAL
Indiana State Bar Association
Indianopolis
(317) 639-5465

SHELTERS AND SAFE HOUSES

ANDERSON
Women's Alternatives
(317) 643-0200

BLOOMINGTON
Middle Way House, Inc.
(812) 336-0846

COLOMBUS
Turning Point
(812) 379-9844

CRAWFORDSVILLE
Family Crisis Shelter of Montgomery Co., Inc.
(317) 362-2030

ELKHART
County Women's Shelter
(219) 294-1811

EVANSVILLE
Albion Fellows Bacon Center
(812) 422-5622

YWCA Battered Women Shelter
(812) 422-1191

FORT WAYNE
YWCA Shelter for Women
(219) 447-7233

GARY
Gary Commision for Women/The Rainbow
(219) 886-1600

HAMMOND
Haven House
(219) 931-2090

INDIANAPOLIS
The Salvation Army Family Service Center
(317) 637-5551

KOKOMO
YWCA Family Intervention Center
(317) 459-0314

LAFAYETTE
Women in Crisis Program
(317) 423-1118

MICHIGAN CITY
Stepping Stone
(219) 879-4615

MUNCIE
A Better Way
(317) 747-9107

NEW ALBANY
Southern Indiana Outreach YWCA Spouse Abuse Center
(502) 581-7222

RICHMOND
Genesis House
(317) 935-3920

SOUTH BEND
YWCA Women's Shelter
(219) 232-9558

TERRE HAUTE
Bethany House/ Catholic Charities of Terre Haute
(812) 232-4978

Council on Domestic Abuse
(812) 232-1736

VINCENNES
Harbor House
(812) 882-7900

WARSAW
The Beaman House
(219) 267-7701

IOWA

COALITIONS
Iowa Coalition Against Domestic Violence
Lucas Building, First Floor
Des Moines, IA 50319
(515) 281-7284

LEGAL
Iowa State Bar Association
Des Moines
(515) 243-3179

PROGRAMS FOR MEN WHO BATTER
Northwest Iowa Mental Health
(800) 242-5105

Estherville Crisis Line
Estherville
(712) 362-4612
Call for a referral.

SHELTERS AND SAFE HOUSES

AMES
Assault Care Center
(515) 232-2303

BURLINGTON
YWCA Shelter and Sexual Abuse Center
(319) 752-4475

CEDAR RAPIDS
YWCA Women's Emergency Shelter
(319) 363-2093

CLINTON
Gateway YWCA, Women's Resource Center
(319) 243-STOP

COUNCIL BLUFFS
Domestic Violence Program
(712) 328-0266

DAVENPORT
Family Resources Domestic Violence Advocacy Programs
(319) 326- 9191

DECORAH
Services for Abused Women
(800) 383-2988
(312) 382-2989

DES MOINES
Family Violence Center
(515) 243-6147

DUBUQUE
YWCA Battered Women Program
(319) 588-4016

ELDORA
Mid Iowa Stepping Stones
(515) 858-2618

ESTHERVILLE
Council for the Prevention of Domestic Violence
(712) 362-4612

FORT DODGE
Family Violence Center of North Central Iowa
(515) 955-5456

IOWA CITY
Domestic Violence Intervention Program
(319) 351-1043

KAEKUK
Tri State Coalition Against Family Violence
(319) 524-4445

MALVERN
Stepping Stones Domestic Abuse Program
(800) HOUSE33

MARSHALLTOWN
Domestic Violence Alternatives, Inc.
(515) 753-3513

MASON CITY
Crisis Intervention Service
(515) 424-9133

MUSCATINE COUNTY
Rape/Assault Care Services
(319) 263-8080

OTTUMWA
Adult Life/Family Crisis Association
(515) 683-3122

PELLA
Turning Point
(800) 433-SAFE

SIOUX CENTER
Domestic Violence Aid Center, Inc.
(712) 737-3307

SIOUX CITY
Council on Sexual Assault and Domestic Violence
(712) 258-7233

WATERLOO
Crisis Services Family Service League
(319) 233-8484

Integregated Crisis Services
(319) 233-8484

KANSAS

COALITIONS
Kansas Coalition Against Sexual & Domestic Violence
820 SE Quincy, #416-B
Topeka, KS 66612
Contact person: Trish Bledsoe
(913) 232-9784

LEGAL
Kansas State Bar Association
Topeka
(913) 234-5696

PROGRAMS FOR MEN WHO BATTER
Domestic Violence Association of Central Kansas
1700 E Iron
Salina, KS 67401
(913) 827-5862
> Call and ask for a referral in your area.

SHELTERS AND SAFE HOUSES

DODGE CITY
Crisis Center of Dogde City
(316) 255-6510

EMPORIA
B.O.S., Inc.
(316) 342-1870

GARDEN CITY
Family Crisis Service's Domestic Violence Program
(316) 275-5911

GREAT BEND
Family Crisis Center
(316) 792-1885

HAYS
Northwest Kansas Family Violence Prevention Program
(913) 625-3055

HUTCHINSON
Reno County Victims of Abuse Network
Sexual Assault/ Domestic Violence Center
(316) 663-2522

IOLA
Family Lifeline, Inc.
(316) 365-4960

KANSAS CITY
Rebbeca Vinscon Center
(913) 321-0951

LAWRENCE
Women's Transitional Care Services
(913) 841-6887

LEAVENWORTH
Alliance Against Family Violence
(913) 682-9131

MANHATTAN
The Crisis Center, Inc.
(913) 539-2785

OVERLAND PARK
Safehouse, Inc.
(913) 262-2868

PITTSBURG
Safehouse, Inc.
(316) 231-8692

SALINA
Domestic Violence Association of Central Kansas
(913) 827-4747

TOPEKA
Battered Women Task Force
(913) 233-1730

WICHITA
YWCA Women's Crisis Center
(316) 267-7233

WINFIELD
Cowley County Safe House
(316) 221-4357

KENTUCKY

COALITIONS
Kentucky Domestic Violence Association
P.O. Box 356
Frankfort, KY 40602
Contact person: Sherry Allen Currens
(502) 875-4132

LEGAL
Frankfort
Kentucky State Bar Association
(502) 564-3795

PROGRAMS FOR MEN WHO BATTER
Transitions
Seven Counties Services, Inc.
200 South 7th Street, #605
Louisville, KY 40202
(502) 584-0044

SHELTERS AND SAFE HOUSES

ASHLAND
DOVES
(606) 784-7980

BEATTYVILLE
Ressurection Home, Inc.
(606) 464-8481

BOWLING GREEN
Barren River Area Safe
(502) 1183

ELIZABETHOWN
Lincoln Trail Domestic Violence Program
(502) 769-1234

HOPKINSVILLE
Sanctuary Inc.
(502) 886-8174

LEXINGTON
The Center for Women & Families
(606) 255-9808

LOUISVILLE
YWCA Spouse Abuse Center
(502) 581-7222

MT. VERNON
Family Life Abuse Center
(606) 256-2724

MURRAY
Spouse Abuse Hotline & Safehouse
(502) 759- 4050

NEWPORT
Women's Crisis Center
(606) 491-3335

OWENSBORO
Owensboro Area Spouse Abuse Shelter
(502) 685-0260

PADUCHA
Purchase Area Spouse Abuse Center
(502) 443-6001

RED FOX
LKLP Spouse Abuse
(606) 439-5129

SOMERSET
Bethany House
(606) 679-8852

LOUISIANA

COALITIONS
Louisiana Coalition Against Domestic Violence
1000 Howard Avenue, #1200
New Orleans, LA 70113
Contact person: Barbara Blunt
(504) 523-3755 Ext. 2923

LEGAL
New Orleans Bar Association
New Orleans
(504) 566-1600

SHELTERS AND SAFE HOUSES

ALEXANDRIA
Turning Point
(318) 445-2022

BATON ROUGE
Capital Area Family Violence Intervention Center
(504) 389-3001

FRANKLIN
CHEZ Hope
(318) 923-4537

LAFAYETTE
Faith House
(318) 232-8954

LAKE CHARLES
Calcasieu Women's Shelter
(318) 436-4552

MONROE
YWCA
(318) 323-1505

NEW IBERIA
Safety Net For Abused Persons
(318) 367-7627

NEW ORLEANS
Crescent House
(504) 486-0377

YWCA Battered Women's Program
(504) 486-0377

SHREVEPORT
YWCA Family Violence Program
(318) 222-2117

MAINE

COALITIONS
Maine Coalition For Family Crisis Services
P.O. Box 89
Winterport 04496
Contact person: Tracy Cooley
(207) 941-1194

Please Don't Let Him Hurt Me Anymore

LEGAL
Maine Bar Association
Augusta
(207) 622-1460

SHELTERS AND SAFE HOUSES

AUBURN
Abused Women's Advocacy
(207) 795-4020

AUGUSTA
Family Violence Project
(207) 623-3569

BANGOR
Spruce Ruth Association
(207) 947-0496

DOVER-FOXCROFT
Womancare/Aegis Association
(207) 564-8401

MACHISE
Womankind Inc.
(207) 255-4785

PRASQUE
Family Support Center Inc.
(207) 769-8251

ROCKLAND
New Hope For Women
(207) 594-2128

SANFORD
Caring Unlimited York Co. Domestic Violence Center
(207) 282-2182

MARYLAND

COALITIONS
Maryland Network Against Domestic Violence
11501 Georgia Avenue, #403
Silver Spring, MD 20915
Contact person: Sue Mize
(301) 942-0900

LEGAL
Maryland State Bar Association
Baltimore
(800) 492-1964

PROGRAMS FOR MEN WHO BATTER
House of Ruth
2201 Asgonne Drive
Baltimore, MD
(410) 889-0840

SHELTERS AND SAFE HOUSES

ANNAPOLIS
YWCA Battered Spouse Counseling & Shelter Program
(410) 222-7273

BALTIMORE
Baltimore House of Ruth Inc.
(410) 889-7884

BETHESDA
Abused Persons Program
(301) 654-1881

COLMAR MANOR
Family Crisis Center, Inc. Of Prince George's County
(301) 864-9101

COLUMBIA
Citizens Against Spousal Assault Of Howard County
(410) 997-2272

CUMBERLAND
Family Crisis Resource Center
(310) 759-9244

DANTON
Mid-Shore Council On Family Violence, Inc.
(410) 822-5276

FREDERICK
Heartly House
(301) 662-8800

HAGERSTOWN
CASA Inc.
(301) 739-8975

PRINCE FREDERICK
Abused Persons Program/Calvert County
(410) 535-1121

WALDORF
Community Crisis & Referral Center, Inc.
(301) 645-3336

MASSACHUSETTS

COALITIONS
Massachusetts Coalition of Battered Women's Service
Groups
210 Commercial Street, 3rd Floor
Boston, MA 02109
(617) 248-0922

LEGAL
Massachusetts Bar Association
Boston
(617) 542-9103

PROGRAMS FOR MEN WHO BATTER
Common Purpose, Inc.
259 Massachusetts Avenue
Arlington, MA 02174

EMERGE
18 Hurley Street
Cambridge
(617) 547-9870

SHELTERS AND SAFE HOUSES
ATTLEBORO
New Hope, Inc.
(508) 695-2113

BOSTON
Casa Myrna Vazquez, Inc.
(617) 521-0100

BROCKTON
Womansplace
(508) 588-2041

CAMBRIDGE
Transition House (Harvard)
(617) 661-7203

CHELSEA
Harbor Me, Inc.
(617) 889-2111

FALL RIVER
Stanley Street Treatment & Women's Resource Center
(508) 675-0087

Please Don't Let Him Hurt Me Anymore

FITCHBURG
Battered Women's Resources, Inc.
(508) 630-1031
Women's Resource Center, Inc.
(508) 342-9355
(508) 342-2919

GREENFIELD
New England Learning Center For Women In Transition
(413) 772-0806

HAVERHILL
Women's Resource Center
(508) 373-4041

HOLYOKE
Womanshelter/Companeras
(413) 536-1628

HYANNIS
Independence House, Inc.
(508) 428-4720

JAMAICA PLAINS
Elizabeth Stone House
(617) 522-3417

LAWRENCE
Women's Resource Center and Latinos Against Sexual Assault
(508) 685-2480

LOWELL
Alternative House
(508) 454-1436

MALDEN
Services Against Family Violence
(617) 324-2221

NEW BEDFORD
New Bedford Women's Center/Battered Women's Project
(508) 992-4222

NEWBURYPORT
Women's Crisis Center
(508) 465-2155

NORTHAMPTON
Necessities/Necesidades
(413) 586-5066

PLYMOUTH
South Shore Women's Center
(508) 746-2664

ROXBURY
Renewal House
(617) 277-4194

SALEM
Help For Abused Women And Their Children
(508) 744-6841

SOMERVILLE
Respond, Inc.
(617) 623-5900

WALTHAM
Waltham Battered Women Support Committee, Inc.
(617) 891-0724
(800) 899-4000

WESTFIELD
New Beginnings
(413) 562-1920

WORCESTER
Abby's House
(508) 756-5486

Daybreak, Inc.
(508) 755-9030

MICHIGAN

COALITIONS

Michigan Coalition Against Domestic Violence
P.O. Box 16009
Lansing, MI 48901
(517) 484-2924

LEGAL

Michigan State Bar Association
Lansing
(517) 372-9030

SHELTERS AND SAFE HOUSES

ADRIAN
Call Some Concerned, Inc.
(517) 263-6737

Family Counseling & Children's Services
(313) 265-6776

ALPENA
Shelter, Inc.
(517) 356-9650

ANN ARBOR
Domestic Violence Project/S.A.F.E. House
(313) 995-5444

BATTLE CREEK
S.A.F.E. Place
(616) 965-7233

BIG RAPIDS
Women's Information Service, Inc.
(616) 796-6600

CADILLAC
Cadillac Area O.A.S .I.S.
(616) 775-7233

CALUMET
Barbara Kettle Gundlach
Shelter Home for Abused Women
(906) 337-5623

COLDWATER
Branch County Coalition Against
Domestic Violence/Shelter House
(517) 278-7432

DETROIT
Interim House
(313) 861-5300

Women's Justice Center/My Sister's Place
(313) 921-3900

FLINT
SAFE House of Flint YWCA
(313) 238-7233

GRAND RAPIDS
YWCA Domestic Crisis Center
(616) 451-2744

GRAYLING
Riverhouse Shelter
(517) 348-8972

HILLSDALE
Domestic Harmony
(517) 439-1454

HOLLAND
Center for Women in Transition
(616) 842-4357

HOWELL
Livingston Area Council Against Spousal Abuse
(313) 227-7100

IONIA
Eight Cap Inc. Ionia/Monhalm Domestic Violence
Program
(616) 527-5252

Spouse Abuse Center
(616) 527-3351

IRON MOUNTAIN
Caring House
(906) 774-1112

IRONWOOD
Domestic Violence Escape (DOVE)
(906) 932-0310

JACKSON
AWARE, Inc.
(517) 783-2861

KALAMAZOO
Domestic Assault Program/YWCA
(616) 385-3587

L'ANSE
Baraga County Shelter Home
(906) 524-5017

LANSING
Council Against Domestic Assault
(517) 372-5572

LAWRENCE
Van Cas Community Action Program
(616) 445-3831 business hours only

LUDINGTON
Region 4 Community Services
Women's Shelter
(616) 845-5808

MANISTEE
CHOICES (Manistee Co. Domestic Violence Prevention
Program
(616) 723-6004

MARQUETTE
Women's Center/Harbor House
(906) 226-6611

MIDLAND
Council on Domestic Violence and Sexual Assault
(517) 835-6771

MONROE
Family Counseling & Shelter Services
(313) 242-7233

MOUNT CLEMENS
Turning Point Inc.
(313) 463-6990

MOUNT PLEASANT
Women's Aid Service, Inc.
(517) 772-9168

MUSKEGON
Every Woman's Place, Inc.
(616) 726-4493

PETOSKEY
Women's Resource Center of Northern MI., Inc. Safe
Home
(616) 347-0082

PONTIAC
Haven-Help Against Violent Encounters Now!
(313) 334-1274

PORT HURON
Domestic Assault/Rape Elimination Services
(313) 985-5538

SAGINAW
Underground Railroad, Inc.
(517) 755-0411

SAINT JOHNS
Relief After Violent Encounter
(517) 224-7283

SAULT SAINT MARIE
R.U.P. Domestic Violence Program
(906) 635-0566

ST. JOSEPH
Safe Shelter
(616) 983-4275

THREE RIVERS
St. Joseph County Domestic Assault Shelter Coalition
(800) 828-2023
(616) 279-5122

TRAVERSE CITY
Women's Resource Center
(616) 941-1210

WESTLAND
First Step
(313) 459-5900

MINNESOTA

COALITIONS
Minnesota Coalition for Battered Women
1619 Dayton Avenue, #3
St. Paul, MN 55104
Contact person: Marcelle Diedrcih
(612) 646-6177

LEGAL
Minnesota Bar Association
St. Paul
(612) 333-1183

PROGRAMS FOR MEN WHO BATTER
Domestic Abuse Intervention Project
206 West Fourth Street
Duluth, MN 55806
(218) 722-2781

SHELTERS AND SAFE HOUSES

AIKEN
Aiken County Women's Advocates
(218) 828-1216

BELLE PLAINE
Southern Valley Alliance for Battered Women
(612) 873-4214

BEMIDJI
Northwoods Coalition for Battered Women
(218) 751-6346

BRAINERD
Women's Center of Mid-Minnesota
(218) 828-1216

BROOKLYN CENTER
Domestic Abuse Intervention Project
(612) 536-1850

CALEDONIA
Houston County Women's Resources
(800) 362-8255
(507) 724-2676

CAMBRIDGE
The Refuge
(612) 689-3532

CHISHOLM
Range Women's Advocates
(800) 232-1300
(218) 254-3377

CIRCLE PINES
Alexandra House
(612) 780-2330

DETROIT LAKES
Lakes Area Service for Rape & Domestic Violence
(218) 847-7446

DULUTH
Women's Coalition
(218) 728-6481

FERGUS FALLS
Women's Crisis Center
(218) 739-3359

GRAND MARAIS
Cook County Collective
(218) 387-1237

GRAND RAPIDS
Advocates Against Domestic Abuse
(218) 326-8565

HOPKINS
Sojouner Shelter for Battered Women
(612) 933-7422

INTERNATIONAL FALLS
Friends Against Abuse
(218) 285-7220

INVER GROVE HEIGHTS
Lewis House
(612) 457-0707

LAKE ELMO
Family Violence Network
(612) 770-0777

MANKATO
C.A.D.A. House Inc.
(507) 625-3966

MARSHALL
Community Intervention Program
(507) 532-2350

MCGREGOR
Aiken County Woments Advocates
(218) 828-1216

MINNEAPOLIS
Crime Victim Center/MN Citizens Council on Crime &
Justice
(612) 340-5400

Domestic Abuse Project
(612) 646-0994

Hariet Tubman Women's Shelter
(612) 827-2841

Incarnation House
(612) 827-5776

Please Don't Let Him Hurt Me Anymore

MORRIS
Stevens County Committee for Battered Women
(612) 589-1481

PARK RAPIDS
Battered Women's Services of Hubbard County, Inc.
(800) 939-2199
(218) 732-7413

PLYMOUTH
Home Free Shelter
(612) 559-4945

ROCHESTER
Women's Shelter Inc.
(507) 285-1010

SAINT CLOUD
Woman's House
(612) 252-1603

ST. PAUL
Casa de Esperanza
(612) 772-1611

Lesbian Battering Intervention Project
(612) 646-0994

Women's Advocate
(612) 227-8284

W.H.I.S.P.E.R.
(612) 646-0994

THIEF RIVER FALLS
Violence Intervention Project
(218) 681-5557

TWO HARBORS
North Shore Horizons
(218) 834-5924

WADENA
S.A.F.E. (Stop Abusive Family Environments)
(218) 631-1714

WILLMAR
Shelter House
(800) 476-3234
(612) 235-4613

WINONA
Women's Resource Center
(507) 452-4440

MISSISSIPPI

COALITIONS
Mississippi Coalition Against Domestic Violence
Biloxi, MI 39533
Contact person: Jane Philo
(601) 436-3809

LEGAL
Mississippi State Bar Association
Biloxi
(601) 948-4471

SHELTERS AND SAFE HOUSES

BILOXI
Gulf Coast Women's Center
(601) 435-1968

COLUMBUS
Safe Haven, Inc.
(601) 327-6040

GREENVILLE
The Salvation Army Domestic Violence Shelter
(601) 334-3249

JACKSON
Shelter for Battered Families
Catholic Charities, Inc.
(601) 366-0222

LAUREL
Domestic Abuse Family Shelter
(DAFS)
(601) 428-8821

MERIDIAN
Care Lodge Domestic Violence Shelter
(601) 693-4673

OXFORD
Domestic Violence Project, Inc.
(601) 234-5085

PASCAGOULA
Salvation Army Domestic Violence Shelter
(601) 762-8267

TUPELO
S.A.F.E., Inc.
(601) 841-CARE

VICKSBURG
Haven House
(601) 638-0555

MISSOURI

COALITIONS
Missouri Coalition Against Domestic Violence
331 Madison
Jefferson City, MO 65101
Contact person: Colleen Cobie
(314) 634-4161

LEGAL

Missouri State Bar Association
Jefferson
(314) 635-4128

PROGRAMS FOR MEN WHO BATTER

RAVEN
6665 Delmar, Suite 302
University City, MO 63130
(314) 645-2075

SHELTERS AND SAFE HOUSES

CAMDENTON
Citizens Against Domestic Violence
(314) 346-2633

COLUMBIA
The Shelter/Comprehensive Human Services, Inc.
(314) 875-1370

FESTUS
Comtrea, Inc.
(314) 942-1376

HANNIBAL
Avenues
(314) 221-4280

INDEPENDENCE
Hope House, Inc.
(816) 461-4673

JEFFERSON CITY
Rape & Abuse Crisis Service
(314) 634-4911

JOPLIN
Lafayette House
(417) 782-7273

KANSAS CITY
N.E.W.S. House for Battered Women
(816) 241-0311

Rose Brooks Center Inc.
(816) 861-6100

SafeHaven
(816) 452-8535

POPLAR BLUFF
Haven House
(314) 686-4873

SEDALIA
CASA (Citizens Against Spouse Abuse, Inc.)
(816) 827-5555

SPRINGFIELD
The Burrell Center
(417) 883-5400

ST. CHARLES
The Women's Center
(314) 946-3257

ST. JOSEPH
YWCA Shelter
(816) 232-1225

ST. LOUIS
ALIVE
(314) 993-2777

St. Martha's Shelter
(314) 533-1313

TRENTON
Trenton Shelter
(816) 359-3297

WARRENSBURG
Survival Center for Abused Adults
(816) 429-2847

WEST PLAINS
Christos House
(417) 256-5759

MONTANA

COALITIONS
Montana Coalition Against Domestic Violence
P.O. Box 5096
Bozeman, MT 59715
(406) 586-7689

LEGAL
Montana State Bar Association
Billings
(406) 245-7990

SHELTERS AND SAFE HOUSES

BILLINGS
The Salvation Army Gateway House
(406) 259-8100

BOZEMAN
Bozeman Area Battered Women's Network
(406) 586-4111

BUTTE
Butte Christian Community Center/Safe Space
(406) 782-8511

DILLON
Women's Resource Center of Dillon
(406) 683-6106

FT. BENTON
Hi-Lines Help for Abused Spouses
(406) 759-5170

GREAT FALLS
YWCA/Marcy Home
(406) 452-1315

HARLEM
Fort Belknap
(406) 353-2933

HELENA
Friendship Center of Helena, Inc.
(406) 442-6800

KALISPELL
Violence Free Crisis Line
(406) 752-7273

LEWISTON
SAVES, Inc.
(406) 538-2281

LIBBY
Lincoln Counnty Women's Help Line
(406) 293-3223

MISSOULA
YWCA Domestic Violence Assistance Center
(406) 542-1944

SIDNEY
Richland County Coalition Against Domesitc Violence
(406) 482-7421

NEBRASKA

COALITIONS
Nebraska Domestic Violence And Sexual Assault Coalition
315 South 9th, #18
Lincoln, NE 68508
Contact person: Sarah O'Shea
(402) 476-6256

LEGAL
Nebraska State Bar Association
Lincoln
(402) 475-7091

SHELTERS AND SAFE HOUSES

BELLEVUE
Family Service Domestic Abuse Program
(402) 444-4433

BENKELMAN
Domestic Violence Task Force
(308) 423-2676

BROKEN BOW
Central Nebraska Task Force on Domestic Abuse & Sexual Assault
(308) 872-5988

CLAY COUNTY
Clay County Task Force
(402) 762-3805

CRETE
Coordinated Intervention System for Domestic Abuse
(402) 826-2332
(402) 826-2728
(800) 777-7332

FREMONT
Domestic Abuse/Sexual Assault Crisis Center
(402) 727-7777

HASTINGS
SASA Crisis Center
(402) 463-4677

KEARNEY
The S.A.F.E. Center
(308) 237-2599

LEXINGTON
Dawson County Parent-Child Center
(308) 324-3040

LINCOLN
Rape/Spouse Abuse Crisis Center
(402) 475-7273

MCCOOK
Domestic Abuse/Sexual Assault Services
(308) 345-5534

NORFOLK
Norfolk Task Force on Domestic Violence & Sexual
Assault
(402) 379-3798

NORTH PLATTE
Rape-Domestic Abuse Program
(308) 534-3495

OGALLALA
SCIP Sand Hills Crisis Intervention Program
(308) 284-6055

OMAHA
The Shelter
(402) 558-5700

PAPILLION
Multi-purpose Center
(402) 345-7273

SCOTTSBLUFF
DOVES (Domestic Violence Emergency Services)
(308) 436-4357

WAYNE
Haven House Family Services Center
(402) 375-4633

NEVADA

COALITIONS
Nevada Network Against Domestic Violence
2100 Capurro Way, #21-1
Sparks, NV 89431
(702) 358-1171

LEGAL
Nevada State Bar Association
Reno
(702) 329-4100

SHELTERS AND SAFE HOUSES

CARSON CITY
Advocates to End Domestic Violence
(702) 883-7654

ELKO
Committee Against Domestic Violence
(702) 738-9454

ELY
Support, Inc.
(702) 289-8808 (connects through Sheriff's office)

FALLON
Domestic Violence Intervention, Inc.
(702) 423-1313

LAS VEGAS
Temporary Assistance for Domestic Crisis Shelter
(702) 646-4981

LOVELOOK
Pershing County Domestic Violence Intervention
(702) 273-7373

MINDEN
Family Support Council of Douglas County
(702) 782-8692

SPARKS
Committee to Aid Abused Women
(702) 358-4150

WINNEMUCCA
Committee Against Family Violence
(702) 623-6429 (connects through Sheriff's office)

YERINGTON
Alternatives to Living in a Violent Environment
(ALIVE)
(702) 463-4009

NEW HAMPSHIRE

COALITIONS
New Hampshire Coalition Against Domestic Violence
And Sexual Violence
P.O. Box 353
Concord, NH 03302
Contact person: Grace Mattern
(603) 224-8893

LEGAL

New Hampshire State Bar Association
Concord
(603) 224-6942

SHELTERS AND SAFE HOUSES

BERLIN
RESPONSE to Sexual & Domestic Violence
(800) 852-3388

CLAREMONT
Women's Supportive Services
(603) 543-0155

CONCORD
Rape & Domestic Violence Crisis Center
(603) 225-9000

CONWAY
Carroll county Against Domestic Violence and Rape
(800) 336-3795

KEENE
Women's Crisis Services of the Monadnock Region
(603) 352-3782

LACONIA
Lakes Region Domestic Violence and Sexual Assault
Program
(603) 524-5835

LEBANON
Women's Information Service (WISE)
(603) 448-5525

LITTLETON
Support Center Against Domestic Violence & Sexual
Assault
(603) 444-0544

MANCHESTER
Women's Crisis Service/YWCA
(603) 668-2299

NASHUA
Rape and Assault Support Services
(603) 883-3044

PLYMOUTH
Task Force on Domestic & Sexual Violence
(603) 536-1659

PORTSMOUTH
A Safe Place
(800) 852-3388
(603) 436-7924

NEW JERSEY

COALITIONS

New Jersey Coalition For Battered Women
2620 Whitehorse
Hamilton Sq. Road
Trenton, NJ 08690
Contact person: Barbara M. Price
(609) 584-8107

LEGAL

New Jersey State Bar Association
Trenton
(908) 249-5000

SHELTERS AND SAFE HOUSES

BELVIDERE
Domestic Abuse and Rape Crisis Center Inc. of Warren
County
(908) 475-8408

BLACKWOOD
Solace/YWCA
(609) 227-1234

BLOOMFIELD
The Safe House
(201) 759-2154

BURLINGTON
Providence House/Willingboro Shelter
(609) 871-7551

ELIZABETH
YWCA of Eastern Union County
(908) 355-4399

FLEMINGTON
Women's Crisis Services
(908) 788-4044

GLASSBORO
People Against Spouse Abuse
(609) 848-5557

HACKENSACK
Shelter Our Sisters
(201) 944-9600

HAZLET
Women's Center of Monmouth County
(908) 264-4111

JERSEY CITY
Battered Women's Program of the YWCA - Jersey City
(201) 333-5700

LAWRENCEVILLE
Womanspace
(609) 394-9000

MORRIS PLAINS
Jersey Battered Women's Services
(201) 267-4763

NEW BRUNSWICK
Women Aware, Inc.
(908) 249-4505

NEWARK
Essex County Family Violence Program
(201) 484-4446

NORTHFIELD
Atlantic County Women's Center "A Place for Us"
(609) 646-6767

SALEM
Salem County Women's Services
(609) 935-6655

TOMS RIVER
Providence House
(908) 244-8259

TRENTON
Womanspace, Inc.
(609) 394-9000

VINELAND
Cumberland County Women's Center
(609) 691-3713

WOODBURY
People Against Spouse Abuse
(609) 848-5557

NEW MEXICO

COALITIONS
New Mexico State Coalition Against Domestic Violence
2339 Wisconsin, NE, Suite F
Albuquerque, NM 87110
Contact person: Ruth Seigal
(505) 246-9240

LEGAL

New Mexico State Bar Association
Santa Fe
(505) 984-6521

PROGRAMS FOR MEN WHO BATTER

Domestic Violence Program
Shelter for Victims of Domestic Violence
1500 Walters
Albuquerque, NM 87102
(505) 247-4219

SHELTERS AND SAFE HOUSES

ALAMOGORDO
C.O.P.E.
(505) 437-2673

ALBUQUERQUE
The Albuquerque Shelter for
Victims of Domestic Violence
(505) 247-4219

CARLSBAD
Carlsbad Battered Families Shelter
(505) 885-4615

CLOVIS
Shelter for Victims of Domestic Violence
(505) 769-0305

FARMINGTON
Family Crisis Center
(505) 325-3549

GALLUP
Battered Families Services, Inc.
(505) 722-7483

HOBBS
Option
(505) 397-1576

LAS CRUCES
La Casa Inc.
(505) 526-9513

Roswell
The Refuge
(505) 624-0666

RUIDOSO
Family Crisis Center
(505) 257-7365

SANTA FE
Esparanza: Shelter for Battered Families
(505) 473-5200

SILVER CITY
El Refugio
(505) 538-2125

TAOS
Battered Women's Project
(505) 758-9888

NEW YORK

COALITIONS
New York State Coalition Against Domestic Violence
Women's Building
79 Central Avenue
Albany, NY 12206
(518) 432-4864

LEGAL

New York State Bar Association
Albany
(518) 463-3200

PROGRAMS FOR MEN WHO BATTER

Vera House
P. O. Box 365
Syracuse, NY 13209
(315) 425-0818
    Call for information.

SHELTERS AND SAFE HOUSES

ALBANY
Equinox, Inc.
(518) 432-7865

Mercy House
(518) 434-3531

AMSTERDAM
Women's Resource & Crisis Center
(518) 842-3384

BATAVIA
Domestic Violence Project of Genesee County
(716) 343-5808

BELMONT
Allegany County Community Opportunities & Rural
Development
(716) 593-5322

BRONX
Aegia-Project Return Fnd.
(718) 733-4443

Please Don't Let Him Hurt Me Anymore

BROOKLYN
Women's Survival Place
(718) 439-1000

House of Mercy
(718) 256-1469

Park Slope Safe Homes Project
(718) 499-2151

BUFFALO
Haven House
(716) 884-6000

Salvation Army Emergency Shelter
(716) 884-4798
(716) 883-9800

YWCA Residence
(716) 884-4761

CANTON
Saint Lawrence Valley
(315) 265-2422

CATSKILL
Columbia-Greene Domestic Violence Program
(518) 943-9211

CORTLAND
Aid to Women Victims of Violence Program-YWCA
(607) 756-6363

DELHI
Delaware Opportunities Inc.
(607) 746-6278

EAST MEADOW
Nassau Co. Coalition Against Domestic Violence, Inc.
(516) 542-0404

ELIZABETHTOWN
End DV Program
(518) 873-9240

ENDICOTT
Advocacy/Support/Alcoholic Program Outreach of SOS Shelter
(607) 754-5174

FAR ROCKAWAY
Transition Center
(718) 327-7660

FREDONIA
AMICAE, Hotline for Rape & Battering
(800) 252-8748

GENESCO
Chances and Changes
(716) 658-2660

GENEVA
Family Counseling Services of the Finger Lakes Inc.
(315) 789-2613

GLOVERSVILLE
Family Violence Project
(518) 725-5300

ISLIP TERRACE
Long Island Women's Coalition, Inc.
(516) 666-8833

ITHACA
Tompkins County Task Force for Battered Women
(607) 277-5000

JAMAICA
Allen Women's Resource Center
(718) 739-6202

Please Don't Let Him Hurt Me Anymore

JAMESTOWN
YWCA Family Violence/Sexual Assault Network
(716) 484-0052

KINGSTON
Family Shelter
(914) 338-2370

LOCKPORT
Lockport YWCA
32 Cottage Street
(716) 433-6716

MANHATTAN
Victims Intervention Project/East Harlem Council for
Human Service
(212) 360-5090

NEW YORK
Henry Street Shelter
(212) 475-6400

New York Asian Women's Center
(212) 732-5230

Project Oasis
(212) 577-7777

Victim Services Agency
(212) 577-7777

Victims Intervention Project
(212) 360-5090

NEWBURGH
Orange County Safe Home
(914) 562-5340

NIAGARA FALLS
Family & Children's Services -Passage Program
(716) 285-6984

NORTH TONAWANDA
YWCA of the Tonawandas Inc.
(716) 692-5643

NORWICH
Domestic Violence Action
(607) 336-1101

ONEIDA
Victims of Violence
(315) 366-5000

ONEONTA
Aid to Battered Women Victims of Violence
(607) 432-4855

OSWEGO
Services to Aid Families
(315) 342-1600

POUGHKEEPSIE
Grace Smith House
(914) 471-3033

ROCHESTER
Alternatives for Battered Women,
(716) 232-7353

YWCA of Rochester & Monroe
(716) 546-5820

SCHENECTADY
Schenectady YWCA Services
(518) 374-3394

SALAMANCA
Cattarangus Community Action Domestic Violence
Program
(716) 945-3970

SARATOGA SPRINGS
Domestic Violence Services
(518) 584-8188

SHIRLEY
Brighter Tomorrows
(516) 395-1800

SPRING VALLEY
Rockland Family Shelter
(914) 425-0112

SYRACUSE
Dorothy Day House
(315) 474-7011

The Salvation Army, Syracuse
(315) 479-1332

Vera House
(315) 468-3260

YWCA Residence
(315) 445-1418

THORNWOOD
Northern Weschester Shelter, Inc.
(914) 747-0707

TROY
Families in Crisis Program of Unity House
(518) 272-2370

UTICA
YWCA Hall House
(315) 797-7740

WARSAW
Wyoming County
(716) 786-3300

WATERTOWN
Jefferson County Women's Center
(315) 782-1855

WHITE PLAINS
Samaritan House
(914) 949-4008

YONKERS
My Sister's Place-Refuge from Domestic Violence
(914) 969-5800

NORTH CAROLINA

COALITIONS
North Carolina Coalition Against Domestic Violence
P.O. Box 51875
Durham, NC 27717
Contact person: Kathy Hodges
(919) 956-9124

LEGAL
North Carolina State Bar Association
Durham
(919) 828-0561

PROGRAMS FOR MEN WHO BATTER
NOVA
1205 Harding Place
Charlotte, NC
(704) 336-4344

SHELTERS AND SAFE HOUSES

ASHBORO
Randolph County Family Crisis Center
(919) 629-4159

ASHEVILLE
Helpmate, Inc.
(704) 254-0516

BOONE
OASIS, Inc.
(704) 262-5035

BREVARD
SAFE of Transylvania County
(704) 885-7233

BRYSON CITY
Swain County & Qualla Boundary, SAFE
(704) 488-6809

BURLINGTON
Famly Abuse Services of Alamance County
(919) 227-6220

CHARLOTTE
The Unlimited Family Services Shelter for Battered
Women
(704) 332-2513

COLUMBUS
Steps to Hope
(704) 894-2340

CONCORD
C.V.A.N. Battered Women's Shelter
(704) 788-2826

DURHAM
Orange/Durham Coalition for Battered Women
(919) 683-8628

ELIZABETH CITY
Albomarle Hopeline
(919) 338-3011

FAYETTEVILLE
Domestic Care Center Violence Program
(919) 323-4187

FOREST CITY
Prevention of Abuse in the Home
(704) 245-8595

GASTONIA
Gastonia County Battered Spouse Shelter
(704) 867-4357

GOLDSBORO
Family & Children's Service of Greater Greensboro, Inc.
Turning Point Division
(919) 274-7316

GREENSVILLE
Pitt County Violence Program
(919) 752-3811

HICKORY
Family Guidance Center First Step Spouse Abuse
Program
(704) 322-1400

JACKSONVILLE
Onalow County Women's Center
(919) 347-4000

KINSTON
SAFE in Lenoir County, Inc.
(919) 523-5573

LENOIR
Shelter Home of Caldwell County
(704) 758-0888

Please Don't Let Him Hurt Me Anymore

LEXINGTON
Davidson County Domestic Violence Services, Inc.
(704) 243-1628

LUMBERTSON
Southeastern Family Violence Center
(919) 739-8622

MANTEO
Outer Banks Hotline
(919) 473-3366

MARION
Family Services of McDowell County, Inc.
(704) 652-6150

MOREHEAD CITY
Carteret County Domestic Violence Program
(919) 247-3023

MORGANTOWN
OPTIONS, Inc.
(704) 438-9444

MOUNT AIRY
Surry Task Force on Domestic Violence
(919) 386-4046

MURPHY
Task Force on Family Violence/ Reach, Inc.
(704) 837-7477

NEW BERN
Coastal Women's Shelter
(919) 638-5995

RALEIGH
Interact
(919) 828-7740

REIDSVILLE
Help, Inc.
(919) 342-3331

SMITHFIELD
Harbor, Inc.
(919) 934-6161

STATESVILLE
Jubilee House Community
(704) 872-3403

SYLVA
R.E.A.C.H. of Jackson County
(704) 586-2458 (connects through Police dispatch)

TAYLORSVILLE
Family Violence Prevention Services
(704) 632-7364

TROY
Women's Crisis Council
(919) 572-3747

WASHINGTON
OPTIONS
(800) 682-0767
(919) 946-3219

WAYNESVILLE
REACH of Haywood County
(704) 456-7898

WHITEVILLE
Citizens Against Spouse Abuse
(919) 642-3388

WILKESBORO
S.A.F.E.
(919) 838-7233

WILMINGTON
Domestic Violence Shelter and Services
(919) 343-0703

WILSON
Wesley Shelter
(919) 237-5156

WINSTON-SALEM
Family Services Center
(919) 723-8125

NORTH DAKOTA

COALITIONS
North Dakota Council On Abused Women's Services
418 E. Rosser Avenue, #320
Bismarck, ND 58501
Contact person: Bonnie Palacek
(701) 255-6240

LEGAL
North Dakota State Bar Association
Bismarck
(701) 255-1404

PROGRAMS FOR MEN WHO BATTER
Domestic Abuse Treatment Program
Fargo, ND
(701) 293-7273
Call and ask for information and referrals.

SHELTERS AND SAFE HOUSES

BEULAH
Mercer County Women's Action & Resource Center
(701) 873-5087
(701) 873-2274

BISMARCK
Abused Adult Resource Center
(800) 472-2911
(701) 222-8370

BOTTINEAU
Bottineau County Coalition
(701) 228-2255

DEVILS LAKE
Safe Alternatives for Abused Families
(701) 662-5050

DICKINSON
Domestic Violence & Rape Crisis Center
(701) 225-4506

GRAFTON
Domestic Violence Progam of Walsh County
(701) 352-3059

GRAND FORKS
Abuse & Rape Crisis Center
(701) 746-8900

JAMESTOWN
Safe Shelter
(701) 251-2300

STANLEY
Action Resource Center
(701) 628-3233

VALLEY CITY
Abused Persons Outreach Center
(701) 845-0072

WILLISTON
Family Crisis Shelter
(701) 572-9111

OHIO

COALITIONS
Action Ohio Coalition For Battered Women
P.O. Box 15673
Columbus, OH 43215
(614) 221-1255

Ohio Domestic Violence Network
65 South 4th Street, #302
Columbus, OH 43215
(614) 784-0023

LEGAL
Ohio State Bar Association
Columbus
(614) 466-2000

PROGRAMS FOR MEN WHO BATTER
Another Way
c/o Every Woman's House, Inc.
225 N. Grand Street
Wooster, OH
(216) 263-1020
    Call for information and referrals.

SHELTERS AND SAFE HOUSES

AKRON
Battered Women's Shelter
(216) 374-1111

ALLIANCE
Alliance Area Domestic Violence
(216) 823-PACE

ASHTABULA
Homesafe
(216) 992-2727

ATHENS
My Sister's Place
(614) 593-3402

BATAVIA
House of Peace, Clermount YWCA
(513) 753-7281

BEACHWOOD
The Center for the Prevention of Domestic Violence
(216) 391-HELP

CANTON
Domestic Violence Project Inc.
(216) 452-6000

CELINA
Family Crisis Network
(419) 586-1133

CHARDON
WomanSafe, Inc.
(216) 564-9555

CHILLICOTHE
Rose County Coalition Against Domestic Violence
(614) 773-4357

CINCINNATI
YWCA - Alice Paul House
(513) 241-2757

CLEVELAND
Templum House
(216) 631-2275

DEFIANCE
Northwestern Ohio Crisis Line Inc.
(419) 782-1100

ELYRIA
Genesis House c/o Center for Children and Youth
(216) 323-3400

FINDLAY
Domestic Violence Shelter of Hancock County/Rape Crisis
(419) 422-4766

FOSTERIA
First Step
(419) 435-7300

GALLIPOLIS
Serenity House, Inc.
(614) 446-5554

GREENVILLE
Shelter from Violence
(513) 548-2020 (connects through Sheriff's office)
Hillsboro

HIGHLAND COUNTY DOMESTIC VIOLENCE TASK FORCE
(513) 393-9904

LANCASTER
The Lighthouse
(614) 687-4423

LIMA
Crossroads Crisis Center
(419) 228-4357

MANSFIELD
The Domestic Violence Shelter, Inc.
(419) 526-4450

MARIETTA
Eve, Inc.
(614) 374-5819

MARION
Concerned Citizens Against Violence Against Women, Inc.
(614) 382-9192

MT. VERNON
New Directions
(614) 397-4357

NEW PHILADELPHIA
Harbor House, Inc.
(216) 343-2778

NEWARK
New Beginnings, Family Counseling Services
(614) 345-4498

OTTAWA
Putnam Family Crisis - Disaster Center
(419) 523-1111

PAINESVILLE
Forbes House
(216) 357-7321

PORTSMOUTH
Southern Ohio Task Force On Domestic Violence
(614) 354-1010

SAINT CLAIRSVILLE
Women's Tri-County Help Center, Inc.
(304) 234-8161 (connects through Sheriff's office)

SPRINGFIELD
Project Woman
(513) 325-3707

STEUBENVILLE
A.L.I.V.E., Inc.
(614) 283-3444

TOLEDO
Bethany House Long Term Shelter
(419) 241-5331

YWCA Battered Women's Shelter
(419) 241-7386

TROY
Family Abuse Shelter of Miami County, Inc.
(513) 335-7148

VAN WERT
Crisis Care Line
(419) 238-4357

WARREN
Contact
(216) 393-1565

WOOSTER
Every Woman's House
(216) 263-1020

XANIA
Greene County Domestic Violence Project
(513) 372-4552

ZANESVILLE
Transitions
(614) 454-3213

OKLAHOMA
COALITIONS
Oklahoma Coalition On Domestic Violence and Sexual Assault
2200 Classen Blvd., #1300
Oklahoma City, OK 73106
Contact person: Georgie Rasco
(405) 557-1210

LEGAL
Oklahoma State Bar Association
Oklahoma City
(405) 524-2365

SHELTERS AND SAFE HOUSES
ADA
Area Services for Battered Women
(405) 436-3504

ALTUS
ACMI House
(405) 482-3800

BARTLESVILLE
Women & Children in Crisis, Inc.
(918) 336-1188

CHICKASHA
Women's Service & Family Resource Center
(405) 222-1819

CLINTON
A.C.T.I.O.N. Associates, Inc.
(405) 323-2604

DURANT
Crisis Control Center
(405) 924-3030

Please Don't Let Him Hurt Me Anymore

ENID
YWCA Option House
(405) 234-7644

IDABEL
Southeastern Oklahoma Services for Abused Women
(405) 286-3369

LAWTON
New Directions, Inc.
(405) 357-2500

MIAMI
Community Crisis Center
(918) 542-1001

MUSKOGEE
Women In Safe Home
(918) 682-7878

NORMAN
Women's Resource Center
(405) 360-0590

POTEAU
Women's Crisis Center
(918) 647-9800

SHAWNEE
Project Safe, Inc.
(405) 273-2420

STILLWATER
Stillwater Domestic Violence Service
(405) 624-3020

TAHLEQUAH
Help In Crisis
(918) 456-4357

TULSA
Domestic Violence Intervention Services
(918) 585-3143

WOODWARD
Northwest Domestic Crisis Services, Inc.
(405) 256-8712

WOODWARD
Woodward Domestic Crisis
(405) 256-1215

OREGON

COALITIONS

Oregon Coaliton Against Domestic Violence
2336 S.E. Belmont Street
Portland 97214
Contact person: Holly Pruett
(503) 239-4486

LEGAL

Oregon State Bar Association
Portland
(503) 620-0222

PROGRAMS FOR MEN WHO BATTER

Domestic Violence Program
Men's Resource Center
2036 SE Morrison
Portland, OR 97214
(503) 235-3433

SHELTERS AND SAFE HOUSES

ASHLAND
Dunn House
(503) 779-4357

ASTORIA
Clatsop County Women's Crisis Service
(503) 325-5735

Please Don't Let Him Hurt Me Anymore

BAKER CITY
May Day, Inc.
(503) 523-5903

BEND
Central Oregon Battering & Rape Alliance (COBRA)
(503) 389-7021

BURNS
HOPE
(503) 573-7176

CLACKAMAS
Clackamas Women's Services
(503) 654-2288

COOS BAY
Coos County Women's Crisis Service
(503) 267-2020

CORVALLIS
Center Against Rape & Domestic Violence
(503) 754-0110

EUGENE
Womenspace
(503) 485-6513

GRANTS PASS
Women's Crisis Suport Team
(503) 479-9349

HILLSBORO
Shelter/D.V.R.C., Inc.
(503) 640-1171

HOOD RIVER
Project Helping Hand Against Violence
(503) 386-6603

KLAMATH FALLS
Klamath Crisis Center
(503) 884-0390

LA GRANDE
Shelter from the Storm DV & Sexual Assault Services
(503) 963-9261

LAKEVIEW
Crisis Intervention Center
(503) 947-2449

LINCOLN CITY
Lincoln Shelter & Services, Inc.
(503) 994-5959

MCMINNVILLE
Henderson House - Family Crisis Shelter
(503) 472-1503

MILL CITY
Canyon Crisis Center
(503) 897-2327

ONTARIO
Project DOVE
(503) 889-2000

PENDLETON
Domestic Violence Services
(503) 278-0241

PORTLAND
Bradley - Angle House, Inc.
(503) 281-2442

Portland Women's Crisis Line
(503) 235-5333

Raphael House of Portland
(503) 222-6222

ROSEBURG
Battered Person's Advocacy
(503) 673-7867

SALEM
Mid Valley Women's Crisis Service
(503) 399-7722

ST. HELENA
Columbia County Women's Resource Center
(503) 397-6161

THE DALLES
Haven
(503) 298-4789

TILLAMOOK
Women's Crisis Center
(503) 842-9486

PENNSYLVANIA

COALITIONS
Pennsylvania Coalition Against Domestic Violence
6400 Flank Drive, #1300
Harrisburg 17112
Contact person: Kelly Dreiss
(717) 545-6400

LEGAL
Pennsylvannia State Bar Association
Harrisburg
(717) 238-6715

SHELTERS AND SAFE HOUSES

ALTOONA
Family & Children's Service of Blair County
(814) 944-3585

BEAVER
Women's Center of Beaver County
(412) 775-0131

BETHLEHEM
Turning Point of Lehigh Valley
(215) 437-3369

BLOOMSBURG
Women's Center
(717) 784-6631

BRADFORD
Bradford Domestic Violence Program
(814) 368-6325

CHAMBERSBURG
Women in Need, Inc.
(717) 264-4444

DUBOIS
Hope for Victims
(814) 371-1223

ERIE
Services for Women, Inc.
(814) 454-8161

GETTYSBURG
Survivors, Inc.
(717) 334-9777

GREENSBURG
Women's Services of Westmoreland County, Inc.
(412) 836-1122

HUNTINGDON
Huntingdon House: A Program for Victims of DV, Inc.
(814) 643-1190

INDIANA
Alice Paul House
(412) 349-4444

JOHNSTOWN
Women's Help Center, Inc.
(814) 536-5361

KITANNING
H.A.V.I.N. Inc.
(412) 548-8888

LANCASTER
Shelter for Abused Women
(717) 299-1249

LEWISBURG
Susquehanna Valley Women in Transition
(717) 523-6482

MCKEESPORT
Womansplace
(412) 678-4616

MEADVILLE
Women's Services, Inc.
(814) 333-9766

MEDIA
Domestic Abuse Project of Delaware County, Inc.
(215) 565-4590

NEW CASTLE
Women's Shelter of Lawrence County
(412) 652-9036

NORRISTOWN
Laurel House
(800) 642-3150

PHILADELPHIA
Women Against Abuse
(215) 386-7777

PITTSBURGH
Crisis Center North
(412) 364-5556

Women's Center Shelter of Greater Pittsburgh
(412) 687-8005

PUNXSUTAWNEY
Crossroads
(814) 849-1617

READING
Berks Women in Crisis
(215) 372-9540

SCRANTON
Women's Resource Center
(717) 346-4671

SHARON
A.W. A.R. E. (Alternatives for Women Advocacy Resources)
(412) 981-1457

STATE COLLEGE
Center County Women's Resource Center
(814) 234-5050

STROUDSBURG
Women's Resources of Monroe County, Inc.
(717) 421-4200

TARENTUS
ALLE-Kiski
(412) 224-HOPE

TOWANDA
Abuse & Rape Crisis Center
(717) 265-9101

UNION CITY
Horizon House Shelter for Women, Inc.
(814) 438-2675

UNIONTOWN
Fayette County Family Abuse Council
(412) 439-9500

Please Don't Let Him Hurt Me Anymore

WARREN
Women's Center—YWCA
(814) 726-1030

WEST CHESTER
Domestic Violence Center of Chester County
(215) 431-1430

WILKES-BARRE
Domestic Violence Service Center
(717) 823-7312

WILLIAMSPORT
Wise Options for Women
(717) 323-8167

YORK
Access- York, Inc.
(717) 846-5400

ZELIANOPLE
Volunteers Against Abuse Center of Butler County, Inc.
(412) 776-6790

PUERTO RICO

COALITIONS
Rev. Judith Spindt
N-ll Calie 11
San Souci
Baymon, PR 00619

SHELTERS AND SAFE HOUSES

ALBERQUE
Hogar Ruth
(809) 883-1884

Casa de Todas
(809) 734-3132

Casa Protegida Julia de Burgos
(809) 781-2570

CAGUES
Casa San Gerado
(809) 746-2827

PARADA
Comision para los Asuntos de La Mujar
(809) 722-2977

SAN JUAN
Casa Providencia
(809) 725-5358

San Vincente de Paul
(809) 772-3744

RHODE ISLAND

COALITIONS
Rhode Island Council On Domestic Violence
324 Broad Street
Central Falls, RI 02863
Contact person: Donna Nesselblush
(401) 723-3051

LEGAL
Rhode Island Bar Association
Providence
(401) 421-5740

PROGRAMS FOR MEN WHO BATTER
Brother To Brother
Center For Non-Violence

389 Charles Street
Providence 02904
(401) 351-1695

Brother To Brother
Cranston
(401) 467-3710
    This number can connect you to other programs in
the state.

SHELTERS AND SAFE HOUSES

CENTRAL FALLS
Blackstone Shelter, Inc.
(401) 723-3057

NEWPORT
Newport County Women's Resource Center
(401) 847-2533

PROVIDENCE
Sojourner House
(401) 431-1870

Women's Center Of Rhode Island, Inc.
(401) 861-2760

WAKEFIELD
Women's Resource Center Of South County
(401) 782-3990

WARWICK
Elizabeth Buffum Chase House
(401) 738-1700

SOUTH CAROLINA

COALITIONS

South Carolina Coalition Against Domestic Violence
And Sexual Assault
P.O. Box 7776
Columbia 29202
Contact Person: Ann Beckham
(803) 254-3699

LEGAL

South Carolina State Bar Association
Columbia
(803) 799-6653

PROGRAMS FOR MEN WHO BATTER

My Sister's House, Inc.
North Charleston
(803) 744-3242
	Call for a referral.

Mens Resource Center
Columbia
(803) 256-0468
	Can refer you to other programs.

SHELTERS AND SAFE HOUSES

AIKEN
Coalition To Assist Abused Persons, Inc.
(803) 648-9900

BEAUFORT
Citizens Opposed To Domestic Violence
(803) 525-1009

COLUMBIA
Sister Care, Inc.
(803) 765-9428

FLORENCE
Pes Des Coalition Against Domestic Violence And
Sexual Assault
(803) 669-4600

GREENVILLE
Family Counseling Center Of Greenville "The Women's
Shelter"
(803) 271-8888

MYRTLE BEACH
CASA
(803) 448-6206

NORTH CHARLESTON
My Sister's House, Inc.
(803) 744-3242

ROCKHILL
Sister-Help
(803) 329-2800

SPARTANBURG
Spartanburg County SAFE Homes Network
(803) 583-9803

SOUTH DAKOTA

COALITIONS
South Dakota Coalition Against Domestic Violence And
Sexual Assault
P.O. Box 689
Agency Village
Contact person: Brenda Hill
(605) 624-5311

LEGAL
South Dakota State Bar Association
Pierre
(605) 224-7554

PROGRAMS FOR MEN WHO BATTER
Citizens Against Rape And Domestic Violence
Men Against Violence Program
P.O. Box 876
Sioux Falls 57101
(605) 339-0116

Help Program For Men Who Batter
Eagle Butte
(605) 964-7233
> Other programs available

SHELTERS AND SAFE HOUSES
ABERDEEN
Resource Center For Women
(605) 226-1212

EAGLE BUTTE
Sacred Heart Center/Women's Shelter
(605) 964-7233

FLANDREAU
Moody County Wholeness Center
(605) 997-3535

FORT THOMPSON
Project Safe
(605) 245-2471

GREGORY
Gregory Shelter
(605) 835-8893

HOT SPRINGS
Crisis Intervention Team
(605) 745-6070

HURON
Huron YWCA Family Violence
(605) 352-9433

LOWER BRULE
Services To Victims Of Crime
(605) 473-5662

MADISON
Madison Area Help Line
(605) 256-3336

MARTIN
People Against Violence
(605) 685-6829

MISSION
White Buffalo Calf Women's Shelter
(605) 856-2317

MITCHELL
Mitchell Area Safehouse
(605) 996-4440

PIERRE
Missouri Shores Women's Resource Center
(605) 224-7187

RAPID CITY
Women Against Violence
(605) 341-4808

REDFIELD
Family Crisis Center
(605) 472-3097

SIOUX FALLS
Children's Inn
(605) 338-4880

Crisis And Transition Shelter/YWCA
(605) 336-3660

WATERTOWN
Women's Resource Center
(605) 886-4300

YANKTON
Contact Center/Women's Center/Shelter
(605) 665-1448

TENNESSEE

COALITIONS
Tennessee Task Force Against Family Violence
P.O. Box 120972
Nashville, TN
Contact person: Kathy England
(615) 386-9406

LEGAL
Tennessee Bar Association
Nashville
(615) 242-9272

PROGRAMS FOR MEN WHO BATTER
Anger Management Program
Family Trouble Center
Memphis
(901) 942-7283

PEACE
211 Union Street, Suite 626
Nashville, TN 37203
(615) 255-0711

SHELTERS AND SAFE HOUSES

ALCOA
Haven House
(615) 982-1087

BRISTOL
Abuse Alternatives, Inc.
(703) 645-7233

CHATTANOOGA
Family And Children's Services
(615) 755-2700

CLEVELAND
Harbor Safe House
(615) 476-3886

COOKEVILLE
Upper Cumberland Alliance Against Violence
(615) 526-4730

CROSSVILLE
Battered Women, Inc.
(615) 484-4642

GALLATIN
Home Safe
(615) 452-4315

JACKSON
Women's Resource And Rape Assistance Program
(800) 273-8712

KINGSPORT
SAFE House
(615) 637-8000

KNOXILLE
Kent C. Withers Family Crisis Center/Child And Family
(615) 637-8000

Serenity Shelter
(615) 971-4673

LAWRENCEBURG
The Shelter, Inc.
(615) 762-1115

MARION
Women's Services Of Family Services
(317) 664-0701

MEMPHIS
YWCA Wife Abuse Services
(901) 458-1661

MORRISTOWN
C.E.A.S.E.
(615) 581-2220

MURFREESBORO
Domestic Violence Program
(615) 896-2021

NASHVILLE
Salvation Army
(615) 242-0411

YWCA Shelter And Domestic Violence Program
(615) 297-8833

NEWPORT
Safe Space/CCADV
(800) 244-5968

OAK RIDGE
CONTACT
(615) 482-0005

TEXAS

COALITIONS
Texas Council On Family Violence
8701 North Mopac, #450
Austin, TX 78759
Contact person: Judy Reeves
(512) 794-1133

LEGAL
Texas Bar Association
Austin
(512) 463-1463

PROGRAMS FOR MEN WHO BATTER
Family Violence Diversion Program
20001 Chicon Street
Austin
(512) 928-9070
    This is a 21 week program. Please call for other referals

SHELTERS AND SAFE HOUSES

ABILENE
Noah Project, Inc.
(915) 676-7107

ALPINE
Rio-Pecos Family Crisis Center
(915) 837-2242

AMARILLO
Rape Crisis/Domestic Violence Center
(806) 373-8022

ANLETON
Women's Center Of Brazoria
(800) 243-5788

ARLINGTON
The Women's Shelter
(817) 460-5568

AUSTIN
Center For Battered Women
(512) 928-9070

BASTROP
Bastrop County Women's Shelter
(512) 321-7755

BAY CITY
Matagorda County Women's Crisis Center
(409) 245-9299

BAYTOWN
Bay Area Women's Center
(713) 422-2292

Brazoria County
Women's Center of Brazoria County
(409) 849-5166

BRENHAM
Faith Mission And Help Center
(409) 830-1488

BROWNSVILLE
Friendship Of Women, Inc.
(512) 544-7412

BRYAN
Phoebe's Home
(409) 775-5355

CLABURNE
Johnson County Family Crisis Center
(817) 641-2322

CORPUS CHRISTI
The Women's Shelter Of The Corpus Christi Area, Inc.
(512) 881-8888

Please Don't Let Him Hurt Me Anymore

DALLAS
Genesis Women's Shelter
(214) 942-2998

The Family Place
(214) 941-1991

DENTON
Denton County Of Friends Of The Family
(817) 382-7273

DUMAS
Safe Place
(806) 935-2828

EL PASO
El Paso Shelter For Battered Women
(915) 7300

FORT WORTH
Women's Haven Of Tarrant
(817) 535-6464

GREENVILLE
Women In Need, Inc.
(903) 454-HELP

HARLINGTON
Family Crisis Center
(512) 9304

HOUSTON
The Roseate, Inc.
(713) 351-4357

HUNTSVILLE
SAFE House
(409) 291-3369

KERRVILLE
Bill County Crisis Council
(201) 257-2400

KILGORE
Kilgore Community Crisis Center
(903) 984-2377

KILLEEN
Families In Crisis, Inc.
(817) 634-8309

LAREDO
Laredo Family Violence Center
(512) 727-7888

LONGVIEW
Women's Center Of East Texas, Inc .
(214) 757- 9308

LUBBOCK
Family Crisis Center
(806) 747-6491

MIDLAND
Permian Basin Center For Battered Women And Their Children
(915) 683-1300

MINERAL WELLS
HOPE, Inc.
(817) 325-1306

NACOGDOCHES
Women' s Shelter Of East Texas
(409) 569-8850

NEW BRAUNFELS
Comal County Women's Center
(512) 620-4357

PAMPA
Tralee Crisis Center For Women
(800) 658-2796

PARIS
Family Haven
(214) 784-6842

PERRYTON
Panhandle Crisis Center
(800) 753-5308

PLANO
Collin County Women's Shelter
(214) 422-7233

RICHMOND
Fort Bend County Women's Refuge Center, Inc.
(713) 342-HELP

SAN ANGELO
ICD Family Shelter
(915) 655-5774

SAN ANTONIO
Women's Shelter Of Bexar County, Inc.
(512) 227-4357

SAN MARCOS
Bays County Women's Shelter
(512) 396-4357

SEGUIN
Quadalupe County Women's Shelter
(512) 372-2780

SHERMAN
Crisis Center
(903) 893-5615

SNYDER
Noah Project West, Inc.
(915) 573-1822 (connects through Police Dept.)

TEXARKANA
Domestic Violence Prevention, Inc.
(903) 793-4357

Tyler
East Texas Crisis Center
(903) 595-5591

THE WOODLANDS
Montgomery County Women's Center
(713) 292-4338

VICTORIA
Women's Crisis Center
(512) 573-HELP

WACO
Family Abuse Center
(817) 772-8999

WITCHITA FALLS
First Step, Inc.
(817) 767-3330

UTAH

COALITIONS
Utah Domestic Violence Advisory Council
120 North 200 West
Salt Lake City, UT 84145
Contact person: Diane Stuart
(801) 752-4493

LEGAL
Utah State Bar Association
Salt Lake City
(801) 531-9077

PROGRAMS FOR MEN WHO BATTER
Paul Olsen
Ogden
(801) 621-3624

Victor Nelson
Logan
(801) 750-7660

Kevin Davis
Logan
(801) 753-5411
All above are groups for men who abuse, call and ask for referals for your area.

SHELTERS AND SAFE HOUSES

LOGAN
Citizens Against Physical And Sexual Abuse
(801) 753-2500

OGDEN
Crisis Center of Northern Utah
(801) 392-7273

PROVO
The Center For Women And Children In Crisis
(8010 377-5500

SALT LAKE CITY
YWCA Of Salt Lake City
(801) 355-2804

VERNAL
Uintah Basin Counseling
(801) 789-5584

VERMONT

COALITIONS
Vermont Network Against Domestic Violence and
Sexual Assault
P.O. Box 405
Montpelier, VT 05601

Contact person: Judy Rex
(800) 223-1302

LEGAL

Vermont State Bar Association
Montpelier
(802) 828-3281

PROGRAMS FOR MEN WHO BATTER

DELTA
Montpelier
(802) 233-2088

Spectrum Program
Burlington
(802) 864-7423

SHELTERS AND SAFE HOUSES

BENNINGTON
PAVE (Protect Against Violent Encounters)
(802) 442-2111

BURLINGTON
Vermont YWCA, Inc.
(802) 862-7520

Women Helping Battered Women
(802) 658-1996

CHELSEA
Chelsea Help For Helping Battered Women
(802) 888-5256

HARDWICK
A.W.A.R.E.
(802) 472-6463

MORRISVILLE
Clarina Howard Nichole Center
(802) 888-5256

MONTPELIER
Battered Women's Services
(802) 223-0855

NEWPORT
Step O.N.E.
(802) 334-6744

RUTLAND
Rutland County Women's Network
(802) 775-3232

SPRINGFIELD
New Beginnings
(802) 885-2050

ST. ALBANS
Abuse And Rape Crisis
(802) 524-6575

VIRGINIA

COALITIONS
Virginians Against Domestic Violence
2850 Sandy Bay Road, #101
Williamsburg, VA 23185
Contact person: Kristi Van Audenhove
(804) 221-0990

LEGAL
Virginia State Bar Association
Richmond
(804) 775-0500

PROGRAMS FOR MEN WHO BATTER

Men Against Violence Against Women
Richmond
(804) 783-2694

(800) 925-2484
Statewide referal line for programs for men who batter

SHELTERS AND SAFE HOUSES

ALEXANDRIA
Alexandria Domestic Violence Program-Office On
Women
(703) 838-4911

Route One Corridor Housing, Inc.
(703) 768-3400

ARLINGTON
Temporary Shelter, Inc.
(703) 237-0881

CARROLTON
The Genieve Shelter
(804) 238-3581

CHARLOTTESVILLE
Shelter For Help In Emergency
(804) 293-8509

CULPEPER
SAFE, Inc. Services To Abused Families
(703) 825-8876

DANVILLE
DOVES, Inc.
(804) 791-1400

DUMFRIES
Turning Points Domestic Violence Program
(703) 221-4951

FREDERICKSBURG
Rappahannock Council On Domestic Violence
(703) 371-1212

FRONT ROYAL
Warren County Council On Domestic Violence
(703) 635-9062

HAMPTON
Virginia Peninsula Council On Domestic Violence
(804) 723-7774

HARRISONBURG
First Step: A Response To Domestic Violence, Inc.
(703) 434-0295

LEXINGTON
Project Horizon
(703) 463-2594

LYNCHBURG
YWCA Family Violence
(804) 528-1041

MARTINVILLE
Rainbow House
(703) 632-8701

NORTON
HOPE House
(800) 572-2728

ONANCOCK
Eastern Shore Coalition Against Domestic Violence
(804) 787-1329

PETERSBURG
CARES, Inc.
(804) 861-0849

PORTSMOUTH
Help And Emergency Response
(804) 393-9449

PUSCELLVILLE
Loudoun Abused Women's Shelter
(703) 777-6552

REDFORD
Women's Resource Center Of The New River Valley
(703) 639-1123

RICHMOND
Domestic Violence Intervention Project
(804) 780-6924

YWCA Women's Advocacy Program
(804) 643-0888

ROANOAKE
The Turning Point
(703) 345-0400

ROCKY MOUNT
Family Resource Center
(703) 483-1234

STANLEY
Choices, Inc. Council On Domestic Violence For Page
County
(703) 743-3733

STAUNTON
Alternatives For Abused Adults
(703) 886-6800

VIENNA
Fairfax County Women's Shelter
(703) 435-4940

WARSAW
Family Focus Of Richmond County, Inc. The Haven
(804) 333-5370

WILLIAMSBURG
AVALON: A Center For Women And Children
(804) 229-7585

WINCHESTER
The Shelter For Abused Women
(703) 667-6466

WASHINGTON

COALITIONS
Washington State Coaltion Against Domestic Violence
200 W Street South East, Suite B
Tumwater, WA 98501
Contact person: Mary Pontarolo
(206) 352-4029

LEGAL
Washington-Bar Association
Seattle
(206) 727-8200

PROGRAMS FOR MEN WHO BATTER
Center for the Prevention of Sexual and Domestic
Violence
1914 North 34th Street, Suite 105
Seattle, WA 98103
(206) 634-1903

Family Services
Northgate
(206) 461-3870

SHELTERS AND SAFE HOUSES

BELLEVUE
Eastside Domestic Violence
(206) 746-1940

BELLINGHAM
Womencare Shelter
(206) 734-3438

BREMERTON
ALIVE
(206) 479-1980

HOQUIAMN
Domestic Violence Center Of Grays Harbor
(800) 562-6025

KELSO
Emergency Support Shelter
(206) 636-8471

MT. VERNON
Skagit Rape Relief/Battered Women's Services
(206) 336-2162

NASELLE
Pacific County Crisis Support Network
(800) 435-7276

NEWPORT
Family Crisis Network
(509) 447-LIVE

OLYMPIA
Safeplace: Rape Relief And Women's Shelter Services
(206) 754-6300

OMAK
The Support Center
(509) 826-3221

PORT ANGELES
Safehome/Sexual Assault Umbrella Community Services
(206) 452-HELP

PORT TOWNSEND
Port Townsend Domestic Violence/Sexual Assault
Program
(206) 385-0321

REPUBLIC
Ferry County Community Services
(509) 775-3132 (connects through Sheriff's office)

RICHLAND
Columbia Basin Domestic Violence Services
(509) 582-9841

SEATTLE
Catherine Booth House
(206) 324-4943

New Beginnings
(206) 522-9472

Women's Resource Center
(206) 461-4882

SHELTON
Recovery: Aid To Victims Of Sexual and Domestic
Abuse
(800) 562-6025

SPOKANE
YWCA Alternatives To Violence
(509) 838-4428

STEVENSON
Skamania County Council On Domestic Violence And
Sexual Abuse
(800) 562-6025

TACOMA
Evergreen Human Services
(800) 562-6025

YWCA Women's Support Shelter
(206) 383-2593

WEST VIRGINIA

COALITIONS

West Virginia Coalition Against Domestic Violence
P.O. Box 85
Sutton, WV 26601
Contact person: Sue Julian
(304) 765-2250

LEGAL

West Virginia State Bar Association
Charleston
(304) 558-7991

PROGRAMS FOR MEN WHO BATTER

Logan Mingo Mental Health Center
Williamson
(304) 235-2954

SHELTERS AND SAFE HOUSES

BECKLEY
Women's Resource Center
(304) 255-2559

CHARLESTON
YWCA Resolve Family Abuse
(800) 352-6513
(304) 340-3550

ELKINS
Women's Aid In Crisis
(304) 636-8433

Please Don't Let Him Hurt Me Anymore

FAIRMONT
Task Force On Domestic Violence
(304) 367-1101

HUNTINGTON
Branches Domestic Violence Shelter
(304) 529-2382

KEYSER
Family Crisis Center
(304) 788-6061

LEWISBURG
Family Refuge Center
(304) 645-6334

MARTINSBURG
Shenandoah Women's Center
(304) 263-8292

MORGANTOWN
Rape And Domestic Violence Information Center, Inc.
(304) 292-5100

PARKERSBURG
The Family Crisis Intervention Center
(304) 428-2333

WESTON
HOPE Inc., Task Force On Domestic Violence
(304) 367-1100

WHEELING
YWCA Abuse Center For Women
(304) 232-0512

WILLIAMSON
Tug Valley Recovery Shelter
(304) 235-6121

WISCONSIN

COALITIONS
Wisconsin Coalition Against Domestic Violence
1051 Williamson Street
Madison, WI 53703
Contact person: Bonnie Brand
(608) 255-0539

LEGAL
Wisconsin State Bar Association
Madison
(608) 257-3838

PROGRAMS FOR MEN WHO BATTER
ONEIDA Tribal Domestic Abuse Program
P.O.Box 265
Oneida, WI 54155
(414) 869-4415
(414) 869-2752
      will refer you to other programs in your locality

SHELTERS AND SAFE HOUSES

APPLETON
Outagamie Company Domestic Abuse Program
(414) 832-1666

BARABOO
Sauk County Task Force
(608) 356-7500

BEAVER DAM
P.A.V.E.
(414) 887-3785

BELOIT
YWCA Family Shelter
(608) 364-1025

EAU CLAIRE
Bolton Refuge House
(715) 834-9578

FOND DU LAC
Friends Aware Of Violent Relationships
(414) 923-1700

GREEN BAY
Family Violence Center
(414) 432-4244

JANESVILLE
YWCA Alternatives To Domestic Violence
(608) 752-2583

KENOSHA
Woman's Horizons, Inc.
(414) 652-1846

LAC DU FLAMBEAU
Lac Du Flambeau Domestic Abuse Program
(715) 7660

LACROSSE
YWCA New Horizons
(608) 791-2600

LADYSMITH
Time-Out Family Abuse Shelter
(715) 532-7089

MANITOWOE
Domestic Violence Center
(414) 684-5770

MARINETTE
Rainbow House
(715) 735-6656

MEDFORD
Taylor Company Citizens Against Domestic Abuse
(715) 748-5140

MERRILL
Haven, Inc.
(715) 536-1300

MILLTOWN
Community Referral Agency, Inc.
(715) 825-4404

MILWAUKEE
Sojourner Truth House
(414) 933-2722

The Milwaukee Women's Center
(414) 671-6140

MONROE
Green Haven Family Advocates, Inc.
(608) 325-7711

NEENAH
Regional Domestic Abuse Services, Inc.
(414) 729-6395

PLATTEVILLE
Family Advocates, Inc.
(608) 348-3838

PORTAGE
Columbia County Advocates For Battered Women, Inc.
(608) 742-7677

RACINE
Women's Resource Center, Inc.
(414) 633-3233

RHINELANDER
Tri-Company Council On Domestic Violence
(715) 362-6800

RICHLAND CENTER
Passages, Inc.
(608) 647-3616

RIVER FALLS
Turning Point For Victims Of Domestic Abuse, Inc.
(715) 425-6751

SAUKVILLE
Advocates Inc. "Friends For Victims Of Abuse"
(414) 284-6902

SHEBOYAN
Safe Harbor
(414) 452-7640

STEVENS POINT
Family Crisis Center
(715) 344-8508

STURGEON BAY
Help Of Door Company, Inc.
(414) 743-8818

SUPERIOR
Center against Sexual And Domestic Abuse
(715) 392-3136

WAUKESHA
Sister House
(414) 542-3828

WAUPACA
Waupaca County Domestic Violence Abuse Task Force
(715) 258-6300

WAUSAU
The Women's Community, Inc.
(715) 842-7323

WEST BEND
Friends Of Abused Families
(414) 334-7298

WISONSIN RAPIDS
Family Center, Inc.
(715) 421-1511

WYOMING

COALITIONS
Wyoming Coalition Against Domestic Violence and
Sexual Assault
341 East E Street, #135A
Casper, WY 82601
Contact person: Judy Logue/Rosemary Bratten
(307) 235-2814

LEGAL
Wyoming State Bar Association
Cheyenne
(307) 632-9065

PROGRAMS FOR MEN WHO BATTER
Women's Self-Help
341 East E Street Suite 135 A
Casper
(307) 235-2814
    Call for other information and referrals.

SHELTERS AND SAFE HOUSES

CASPER
Women's Self Help Center
(307) 235-2814

CHEYENNE
Safe House/Sexual Assault Services, Inc.
(307) 637-7233

CODY
Crisis Intervention Services
(307) 527-7801

DOUGLAS
Converse Co. Coalition Against Family Violence and
Sexual Assault
(307) 358-4800

ETHETE
Circle of Respect
(307) 332-7046

EVANSTON
Uinta County Sexual Assault Family Violence Task
Force
(307) 789-7315

GILLETTE
Gillette Abuse Refuge Foundation
(307) 686-8070

JACKSON
Teton County Task Force On Family Violence/Sexual
Assault
(307) 733-7466

KEMMERER
The Turning Point, Lincoln County Self-Help Center
(307) 877-9209

LARAMIE
SAFE Project
(307) 745-3556

LUSK
Helpmate Crisis Center
(307) 334-2608

NEWCASTLE
FOCUS
(307) 746-3630

RAWLINS
Carbon County COVE
(307) 324-7144

RIVERTON
Office On Family Violence
(307) 856-4734

ROCK SPRINGS
YWCA-SASH (Sweetwater Advocacy And Safe House
(307) 382-6925

SHERIDAN
Women's Center
(307) 672-3222

SUNDANCE
Crook County Family Violence & Sexual Assault Services
(307) 283-2620

THERMOPOLIS
Hot Springs
(307) 864-2131

ORRINGTON
Goshen County Task Force On Family Violence &
Sexual Assault
(307) 532-2118

Please Don't Let Him Hurt Me Anymore

WHEATLAND
Project Safe
(307) 322-4794

WORLAND
Community Crisis Service
(307) 347-4991

NATIONAL LISTINGS

CHILDREN
Child Care Aware
(800) 424-2246
　　National line to help you locate quality child care in your area.

Children's Defense Fund
122 C Street NW, Suite 400
Washington, DC 20001
(202) 628-8787

Child Find of America
(800) 426-5678
24 hours.

Child Help U.S.A.
(800) 422-4453
　　Provides crisis services, referrals and counseling to victims of child abuse. 24 hrs.

Child Support Collecting Services
(800) 736-6272

National Center for Missing and Exploited Children
800-THE-LOST

National Council on Child Abuse and Family Violence
1155 Connecticut Avenue NW, Suite 400
Washington, DC 20036
(800) 222-2000

Runaways Hotline
(800) 621-4000

DEPRESSION

National Foundation for Depressive Illness
P.O. Box 2257
New York, New York 10116
(800) 248-4344

National Institute of Mental Health
5600 Fishers Lane
Room 14C-02
Rockvville, MD 20857
(800) 421-4211

LEGAL

National Center for Women and Family Law
799 Broadway
Room 402
New York, New York 10003
(212) 674-8200
    Legal help, advocates, education and referrals.

National Center for Youth Law
1662 Mission Street, 5th Floor
San Francisco, CA 94103
(415) 543-3307

Please Don't Let Him Hurt Me Anymore

National Clearinghouse for the Defense of Battered
Women
Philadelphia, Pennsylvania
(215) 351-0010

National Women's Law Center
1616 P Street NW, Suite 100
Washinton, DC 20036
(202) 328-5160

NOW Legal Defense and Education Fund
99 Hudson Street
New York, NY 10013
(212) 925-6635

MAIL ORDER BOOK SERVICES

BOOK CALL
800-AL-BOOKS
    Will ship anywhere in the world. 24 hours. Seven
days a week.

Feminist Bookstore News
2358 Market Street
San Francisco, Ca. 94114
(415) 626-1556
    Ask for information.

For Women Only Books
13479 Howard Rd.
Millfield, Ohio 45761
    Write for their catalogue.

Sisterhood Bookstore
1351 Westwood Blvd.
Los Angeles, Ca. 90024
(310) 477-7300

MEDICAL HEALTH
American Medical Association
515 North State Street
Chicago, Illinois 60610
(312) 464-4400

American Medical Women's Association
801 North Fairfax Suite 400
Alexandria, VA 22314
(703) 838-0500
　　　Organized dedicated to the improvement of health care for women. Stresses domestic violence and reproductive rights among others. 12,000 members—medical students and phsycians.

National Women's Health Network
1325 G Street NW
Washington DC 20005
(202) 347-1140
　　　Membership organization for consumers and providers.

Family Health Resource Program on Domestic Violence
(800) 313-1310

AIDS Information Tape
(800) 342-2437

National Association of People with AIDS
(202) 898-0414

National Women's Health Resource Center
Columbia Hospital for Women Foundation
244 M Street Suite 325
Washington, DC 20037
(202) 293-6045

MONEY

National Coalition for Low-Income Housing
1012 14th Street, Suite 1500
Washington, DC 20005
(202) 662-1530

Aid to Families with Dependent Children and Food
Stamps
(800) 252-9330

National Newtwork of Women's Funds
1821 University Avenue Suite 409N
St. Paul, MN 55104
(612) 641-0742
     Primarily educates and supports women's projects.
Also education, program development and research.
Newsletter.

Woman's World Banking
8 West 40th Street
10th Floor
New York, New York 10018
(212) 768-8513.
     Call for an affiliate in your area. Provides training
and credit for low-income women entrepreneurs in their
local communities. Can request written information.

NETWORKS

Displaced Homemakers Network
1531 Pennsylvania Avenue SE
Washington, DC
(202) 467-6346

National Council for Research On Women
Publication Division
530 Broadway, 10th Floor
New York, New York 10012-3920
(212) 274-0730
Networking directories available.

Women's Information & Exchange
National Women's Mailing List
P.O. Box 68
Jenner, CA 95450
(707) 632-5763
Provides computerized information. Mailing lists. Feminist organizations. Their book, "The Women's Information Exchange National Directory" available nationwide in bookstores. $10.00

National Organization for Women
1000 16th St. NW, Suite 700
Washington, DC 20036
(202) 331-0066

PROGRAMS FOR MEN WHO BATTER

National Coalition Against Domestic Violence
10212 14th Street, N.W., Suite 807
Washington, D.C. 20005
(202) 638-6388
Nationwide Referrals

RAVEN
6665 Delmar, Suite 302
University City, MO 63130
(314) 645-2075
    Nationwide Referrals

SHELTERS AND SAFE HOUSES

National Coalition Against Domestic Violence
10212 14th Street, N.W., Suite 807
Washington, DC 20005
(202) 638-6388
    Provides nationwide referrals to shelters and their services for battered women and their children.

SUBSTANCE ABUSE

Narcotics Anonymous World Service Office
P.O. Box 9999
Van Nuys, Ca. 91409
(818) 780-3951
    Groups throughout the country. Twelve-step and self-help.

National Asian Pacific Families Against Substance Abuse
420 East 3rd Street
Suite 909
Los Angeles, Ca. 90013
(213) 413-1096

National Association of Children of Alcoholics
11426 Rockville Pike Suite 100
Rockville MD 20852
(301) 468-0985

National Council on Alcohol and Drug Dependence
1511 K Street NW, Suite 926
Washington, DC 20005
(202) 737-8122

National Institute of Drug Abuse
11426 Rockville Pike
Rockville, MD 20052
(301) 443-6245

National Women's Christian Temperance Union
1713 Chicago Avenue
Evanston, Ill 60201
(708) 864-1396
Headquarters. For women of all faiths.

800-COCAINE
P. O. Box 100
Summit, NJ 07901
Call for a referral to a local hotline.

THERAPY
American Association for Marriage and
Family Therapists
1717 K Street N.W. Suite 407
Washing D.C. 20006
(202) 452-0109
Will give referrals of their members.

American Family Therapy Association
2020 Pennsylvania Ave. N.W. Suite 273
Washington, D.C. 2006
(202) 994-9000
Will refer members in your area.

American Psychological Association
1200 17 Street N.W.
Washington DC 20036
(202) 336-5500
    Will refer you to your state branch office. They in
turn will provide a list of psychologists in your area.

American Psychiatric Association
1400 K. St. N.W.
Suite 1050
Washington DC 20005
(202) 682-6000

National Mental Health Association
1021 Prince Street
Alexandria, VA 22314
(703) 684-7722
    To find an individual therapist in your locality, call
this office and they will refer you to its local affiliate chapter.

VICTIM ASSISTANCE

National Victim Center
2111 Wilson Blvd., Suite 300
Arlington, VA 22201
(703) 276-2880
800-FYI-CALL
    Information clearinghouse.

National Organization for Victim Assistance
1757 Park Road NW
Washington, DC 20010
(202) 232-6682
    Committed to the recognition of victim's rights.

SELF-DEFENSE

National Clearinghouse on Battered Women's Self-Defense
524 McKnight Street
Reading, PA 19601
(215) 373-5697

National Clearinghouse on Marital and Date Rape
Women's History Research, Inc.
2325 Oak Street
Berkeley, California 94708
(510) 524-1582

This book was loved into life...